Jamestown Adventure

Other Books by Olga W. Hall-Quest

HOW THE PILGRIMS CAME TO PLYMOUTH

SHRINE OF LIBERTY: THE ALAMO

JAMESTOWN ADVENTURE

By OLGA W. HALL-QUEST

Illustrated by James MacDonald

E. P. DUTTON & COMPANY, INC.

PUBLISHERS • 1950 • NEW YORK

To the memory of my father

WILLIAM SHAW WILBOURNE

Table of Contents

Jamestown Adventure

CHAPTER I   *Jamestown Rediscovered*

A LONE CYPRESS stands straight and tall in the waters of a broad river some distance from the banks of a green island. It stands as nature's monument to the great adventure that began more than three hundred years ago on what is today the most historic site in the United States—old Jamestown, the first permanent English colony on the shores of the New World.

Long years ago this old cypress stood on the island itself, but the waves lumbered in over the wide reaches of the river and washed away tons of soil. Twenty acres of the island at its western end had been carried out to sea by the tides before a protecting sea-wall was built.

Just as the solitary cypress is no ordinary tree, so the river in whose bed it has so long been rooted is unique compared to most rivers. It is really no river at all, except in appearance and name, but one of the long inlets, or tidewater arms, of Chesapeake Bay. It is one of Virginia's tidal rivers. These brackish tidal rivers do not flow into the sea as fresh-water rivers do, but flow up from the great Bay under tidal pressure from the ocean. Four of these rivers water the broad, flat plain of the eastern side of triangular-shaped Virginia. Two of them still bear their old Indian names—the Rappahannock and the Potomac. The old Pamunkey became the York up to present-day West Point, but beyond this town it is still known by its original Indian name. The name of the Powhatan River was permanently changed to the James. It was up the Powhatan that the English colonists sailed, and they gave to the river and their little settlement on its banks the name of James in honor of their sovereign, King James I of England.

Jamestown was not quite an island at the time these intrepid voyagers landed here. A narrow isthmus connected it with the mainland, but it was so nearly surrounded by water that from the first it was spoken of as James Island. The narrow neck of the peninsula, over which once ran the "Greate Roade," has long since been washed away by the tides, and Jamestown is now, properly speaking, an island. A green, swampy island of fifteen hundred acres, it is about three miles in length and, in its natural setting, little changed from what it was almost three hundred and fifty years ago when the first settlers strove to establish a foothold here.

Today Jamestown lies beautiful and serene, unshadowed by its tragic past. But here it was that the American nation was begun by the venturesome Englishmen who struggled and died, so many of them, fighting famine, yellow fever, bubonic plague, cholera, dysentery, malaria and Indians. It was the island itself that brought death and misery to great numbers, for the malaria-breeding swamps were as deadly as the hostile Indians who lurked in the tall grasses and reeds of the marshlands.

The colonists could not have chosen a more unhealthful site. They had been counseled in England not to select a low, damp place for their habitation. But they had also been ordered not to settle too near the coast, for the Spanish were already on the prowl along the Virginia capes, greedily hunting for the treasures of the New World and on the look-out for Englishmen who were also fortune-hunting. There was little time for three small English ships to explore the maze of tidal waterways. The ocean voyage had been long and exhausting, and the eager venturers were impatient to leave the cramped quarters of the ships and stretch their sea-weary legs on the shores of a new homeland.

So the three little ships headed up the James with all on board scanning the river banks for a promising site far from the sea and the keen-eyed Spaniards who manned the roving galleons. Weary and sick of the sea, they chose a strip of land so swampy that more than half its area was unfit for habitation and where no settler's home would ever be more than a hundred yards from a stagnant, mosquito-infested swamp.

Looking down upon the island from the air today, the light green marshes of Jamestown are seen curving in a lovely serpentine design, but many of them are straight aisles that cut across flat meadow lands or open up far, reedy vistas between tall pines that wall them in on either side. Scientists call these narrow marshways "slashes."

The Jamestown settlers gave the slashes and the marshes names suggested by one thing and another in their experience. And they are known today by those same names that have been preserved in the old records. Up in the northwestern corner of the island lies triangular Back River Marsh, fronting upon the Back River that is Jamestown's curving water boundary on the north that separates it from the mainland. The old Pitch and Tar Swamp snakes its way right through the middle of the island from the northeast to the southwest. And down the island, on what was the site of the original settlement, Gallows Swamp is a sinister reminder that not all the early settlers starved to death, died of disease or were killed by the Indians. Some of them were hanged in the "Public Garden" of the town on the gallows that gave the near-by swamp its name. Largest of all the swamps is a great marshy area named Goose Hill, which is no hill at all, and the "goose"—well, that's puzzling too. It is today an almost impenetrable, pathless region, but long ago rude dwellings stood where solid ground could be found.

No ruins of the earliest Jamestown buildings stand on the island today. Though the colonists sometimes referred in their records to the settlement as "James

City," it was never larger than a small town or village. At the height of its development, around 1676, there were not more than fifty or sixty buildings. Most of them, during this later period, were of brick, and the foundations of some of these old brick houses have been uncovered, but no traces of the earliest settlement have as yet been found. As the old families, the "ancient settlers," moved away the buildings were torn down, burned or simply fell in decay. The shadows gathered and deepened, and the original site of Jamestown that was the birthplace of this nation became a whispering ghost town of the past. James City was forgotten.

Then one day in the year 1857 an artist-writer named Benton Lossing happened upon the scene astride his old horse Charley. He was not interested in the onward push of civilization—he was looking for the long-neglected historic sites in Virginia. The desolation and decay that met his eye that day in old Jamestown shocked him. But it was the sight of the island itself being slowly carried out to sea by the tides that stirred Lossing to an impassioned plea for action. "Look to it, Virginians," he cried, "and let a wall of masonry along the river margin attest your reverence for the most historical relic within your boundaries."

It was not the right time to make a plea for saving what was left of an abandoned site, no matter how historic. The nation that had been born here among the swamps and marshes beside the sparkling waters of the James was falling apart. In 1861 war between the states began and for four long years the North and the South fought against each other on bloody battlefields. Even forgotten Jamestown was briefly occupied when, by order of General Robert E. Lee, a Confederate fort was built near the old church tower, but the fighting passed it by, and in 1865 the tragic war came to an end.

At long last Virginians gave heed to Benton Lossing's warning. They began to think about the historic places within their boundaries that belonged to the vanished past. In 1889 the Association for the Preservation of Virginia Antiquities was chartered and four years later this organization acquired title to twenty-two acres of land on James Island. Old Jamestown had been rediscovered and the work of restoration and preservation went steadily forward. In 1900-1901 the concrete seawall that was so vitally necessary for checking the erosion along the southern shores of the island was built by the United States Government. And in 1907 the great stone obelisk known as Tercentenary Monument was erected to commemorate the three hundredth anniversary of the founding of Jamestown.

But what of that first little palisaded settlement called James Fort? Not only had the wooden palisades and the flimsy buildings within long since vanished, but the very site on which they were built was for a long time unknown. It was not until fairly recently that old records were brought to light which gave evidence that the first settlement, called Old Town, was over half a mile down the river from Brick Church. It can only be conjectured from meager information what those earliest buildings were probably like in appearance. Brick Church, near which Tercentenary Monument stands, is on the site that came to be known as New Town after 1623 when the settlers began moving into more substantial buildings erected both east and west of the church. Old Town was abandoned and forgotten.

It is on the site of old "New Towne" that visitors who now daily throng the island stand and look up at the ivy-covered walls of the ancient church tower. But the tower no longer stands like a gaunt skeleton, desolate and neglected. As in the far-away past, it is now the entrance to a church—the Memorial Church that was built in 1907 over the foundations and chancel of the original building of 1639-1647. Inside, the old cobblestone foundations that long ago supported the wooden structures that preceded the brick edifice can be seen. And in the peaceful graveyard that surrounds the church, the dead who were once Jamestown's first citizens and the progenitors of distinguished Virginia families sleep on in tombs and beneath headstones that have become so mouldy and crumbly with age that it is difficult to decipher their names and epitaphs.

The Relic House is near-by where a fascinating wealth of historical artifacts is on display. It is underground, not above ground, that old Jamestown is being rediscovered and brought to light. This work is being carried on by the Jamestown Archaeological Project that was set up after the rest of the island was acquired by the United States Government in 1934. Digging into the past with spade and shovel, the Project has unearthed the foundations of the first and last State Houses, the last governor's "country house" and the houses of a number of prominent citizens. And the paths by which they went to and fro—faint or strong traces of old streets, walks, lanes, highways. Slowly the outlines of the past are becoming sharp and clear.

And there are not only nature's memorials—tree and swamp and river—but the markers, monuments and tablets that man has set up to commemorate the past and through which the present speaks to the past. A simple stone honors the memory of the Reverend Robert Hunt who administered the first communion of the Anglican Church in America in June, 1607. None, however, takes such hold upon the imagination as do the statues of an Indian maiden and a great soldier of fortune. Pocahontas, the Indian princess, stands among the trees and the shrubbery shading her eyes with her hand as she looks into a future that carried her far from the council fires of her father, the great Powhatan—as far as the court life of England. But Pocahontas will forever be remembered, first and last, perhaps, as the little Indian maiden who became the dear friend of the great Captain and served the English colony so faithfully.

Captain John Smith, sculptured in great cape, bloused trousers and huge boots, stands close-by. Left hand on sword hilt, as though ready for instant action, he gazes down the broad river up which he had sailed that historic day in May, 1607. Such were the far-flung interests and adventures of this great Englishman that he could hardly be called a man with a country. But nowhere does it seem more fitting for his statue to stand than here on the island where he worked and fought and helped to plant the first enduring English settlement.

In time there will be other monuments and statues to honor the men and women of old Jamestown. But those who can look far and deep into the past can see ship after ship breasting the waters of the James, bringing to these shores many men and women to whom no monuments will ever be erected, but each of whom did his and her part in transplanting something of England upon American soil that flourished and in time became —America.

CHAPTER II *The Adventure Begins*

ON THE NIGHT of April 21, 1607, three little ships were caught in a raging tempest somewhere out upon the dark, turbulent waters of the Atlantic beyond the shores of the New World.

No doubt Captain Christopher Newport, in command of the one hundred-ton *Sarah Constant* and leader of the little fleet, prayed, "God save us!" No doubt Captain Bartholomew Gosnold, aboard his own ship the *Goodspeed*, sixty tons lighter, prayed too. And for certain their chaplain, the Reverend Robert Hunt, was in close and earnest converse with God all that black, stormy night. But the captain of the little twenty-ton pinnace, the *Discovery*, was moved to anger rather than to prayer. Captain John Ratcliffe was muttering and growling, as he grasped the railing at shipside to keep from being washed overboard, "Fools—fools all of them! If they had listened to me we'd be safely on our way back to a safe country."

It had been four months since the ships had sailed away from the shores of England—about ten days since they had left the West Indies taking a northerly course in search of a strange land called Virginia. Anxious, trying days, for the mariners admitted they were off their course, that somehow they had missed their reckoning. Wearied by the long voyage, the men had paced their cramped quarters restlessly. There were about one hundred and sixty of them crowded together on the three little ships. The captains had studied their maps and charts and debated what should be done. Finally Captain Ratcliffe had impatiently urged that they turn back. "We'll never reach this wild land," he had said irritably. "Let's give up this foolhardy venture and return to God's own country." But the answer from Newport and Gosnold had been a grim, dogged "No!"

So it was that the *Sarah Constant*, the *Goodspeed* and the *Discovery* rode out the storm that night with furled sails. And another day broke on the wide ocean, but still there was no sign of land. Hopefully, the leadsmen dropped their lead-lines beneath the heavily rolling waves to sound for depth, but it was down, down, down and still no bottom. It was the same on the following two days. On April 25th the grim routine was repeated for the fourth time and the leadsman reported glumly to Captain Newport, "No ground at one hundred fathoms, Sir."

There was mounting tension on board the crowded ships. Tempers were short and even Newport and Gosnold scanned the far reaches of the ocean with tense, worried faces. Night brought welcome relief from the long day of strained watching and waiting and, uncomfortable as they were, the men must have been sleeping soundly and heavily in the early hours of the morning of April 26th. The light of another day was breaking over the waters at four o'clock on that morning when a long, rolling, chanting cry rang out from one of the crow's nests. It roused the sleeping men, brought them stumbling unbelievingly to their feet. Surely—but before they could finish the thought that they had been dreaming, the chant—strong, clear and joyful—rang out again: "La-a-nd Ho-o!! La-a-nd Ho-o!! Land! Land! La-a-nd Ho!!" No modern voyager will ever know the lifting sweetness of that cry, that chant from the lookout coign of a sailing vessel which announced to early adventurers upon the high seas the sighting of land long-looked-for!

The men aboard the *Sarah Constant*, the *Goodspeed* and the *Discovery* had at long last sighted the land of Virginia. And on that day, April 26, 1607, they sailed into Chesapeake Bay and found sheltered anchorage on the leeward side of a cape which Newport named Cape Henry in honor of King James's eldest son. The opposite point he named Charles after the Duke of York.

The Jamestown adventure really began several years earlier when Captain Bartholomew Gosnold had set in motion the current of events which had led to this momentous landing on the shores of Virginia. He was an old sea-dog with an unquenchable thirst for adventure and he was a man of vision as well. In 1607 he was no stranger to the New World. He had already achieved lasting fame when, in May, 1602, he planted a colony on one of the Elizabeth islands south of Cape Cod. It was abandoned after twenty-five days, but it was the first English settlement on the coast of New England, and the islet on which it stood is now called Gosnold Island. A memorial tower has been erected there in his honor.

But the dream of planting English colonies in the New World had been in the hearts of Englishmen for a long time. The coast of Newfoundland was visited by English fishermen as early as 1517, and in 1522 English houses were built here for their accommodation.

The French, the Portuguese and the Spanish were there, too, fishing off the Grand Banks. The Spaniards had already begun to plant colonies when Sir Humphrey Gilbert founded an English settlement at St. John's Port in Newfoundland in 1583. Just how long it survived nobody knows, but it is the first known English colony in America.

About the same time Sir Humphrey's more famous half-brother, Sir Walter Raleigh, was pushing ahead with colonization plans of his own. In 1584 he was given a charter by Queen Elizabeth for the exploration and occupation of a great area of the eastern coast of America which he named Virginia in honor of the Virgin Queen.

Roanoke Island, off the coast of what is now North Carolina, was the site of Raleigh's first settlement in the new country. Tragedy stalked the little colony from the beginning, and the last group of colonists, the straggling survivors of four expeditions, disappeared sometime after 1587 never to be seen again by a white person, and henceforth spoken of as the "Lost Colony."

Such was the heroic spade-work of those who tried and failed. Bartholomew Gosnold returned to England, after his own failure to found a permanent settlement, still fired by dreams of colonizing America. He knew the time was ripe for a great period of discovery and exploration. Elizabeth was dead and James I had ascended the throne. The wars with Spain and the Netherlands had been fought and finished and the restless and the adventurous were eager for new worlds to conquer.

America beckoned as a hope, which Columbus had not extinguished, of finding a new way to Asia. As a land where great riches, particularly in precious metals, were to be found. As a heathen country where the Christian religion could be imparted to the benighted savages. But the most compelling reason for turning the thoughts of Englishmen toward America was the fact that their old enemy Spain was already there—in a dozen or more little mission towns scattered over the present states of South Carolina, Georgia and Florida. Names like Saint Augustine, Orista, San Pedro and Tolomato were dotting what had been nothing but a land of strange Indian names. There had even been a Spanish mission on the shores of Chesapeake Bay in 1570.

Yes, the time was ripe, and for several years after his return from the New England venture Gosnold worked feverishly trying to interest all and sundry in his schemes for making yet another attempt to conquer and tame the wilderness and the wild savages of America.

He talked of America to his friends as a promised land. He talked to the well-born "gentlemen," men who belonged to England's landed gentry—men of influence and means. He gained access to lords and nobles and talked eloquently and persuasively of the glory and the fame that a successful expedition would bring to them and to their country. He sought out the young bloods of the land, the young men of all classes who, like himself, thirsted for adventure. To them he talked for hours of his own exciting experiences on the high seas and in the strange, far-off land of America.

And then he talked to the merchants, but not of adventure. Profits was what interested the hard-headed business men of England, and Gosnold could bring a gleam to their eyes when he told them of the rich resources that would be gathered and unearthed in the virgin country and sent back to them—shiploads of raw materials for manufacture, sale and export. He realized that the time had come for organized companies to take over. Individual initiative and enterprise were not enough for the founding of permanent settlements. And the money for such undertakings would have to come from the rich merchants.

At last Bartholomew Gosnold's long and tireless efforts at promoting America were rewarded. The great London Company—an association of merchants, "gentlemen," and noblemen—was organized. These men of the London Company were called "adventurers"—the merchant and the gentlemen-adventurers who would provide the money for the ships and the supplies necessary to send colonists to America. In return they hoped to wax prosperous from the sale of products that the real adventurers, the settlers, would ship back to England.

Permission was straightaway given the London Company by King James to settle Virginia, and on April 10, 1606, the charter of Virginia was granted. At that time Virginia was a country considerably larger in extent than the present state of Virginia. It extended roughly from present Halifax in Nova Scotia to present Columbia in South Carolina, and the charter provided for the establishment of a company with two branches, one to govern the colony in Southern Virginia and the other, the colony in Northern Virginia.

The London Company, which was to send out the first colony to South Virginia, was given a set of instructions which served as a constitution and was issued by authority of the King. It was specifically stated that the Church of England was to be maintained and that the colonists were "to treat the natives kindly and use all proper means to draw them to the true knowledge and love of God." They were also instructed in the selection of a site for settlement, in the exploration of the region, and informed that the main purposes of their journeys of exploration were to be the search for precious metals and a way to the South Sea. The armchair adventurers in London were looking for quick and fabulous returns on their investment!

Finally three little ships were outfitted for the long voyage. But no women came aboard the *Sarah Constant*, the *Goodspeed* and the *Discovery*. This was an all-man expedition—about one hundred and sixty in number, of whom one hundred and four were the emigrants. About half were "gentlemen"—fine gentlemen whose hands had never been blistered from swinging an axe and who had never planted a row of corn in their lives or had experience of any sort in manual labor. For them was the lure, the gleaming promise and the bright vision that had brought them aboard ship in high-hearted spirits. Before them was the prospect of quick-and-easy riches from the gold they expected to find. There were a few laborers and a few mechanics among them, but not nearly enough, and the rest were soldiers and servants.

The Company had been wise in selecting Captain Christopher Newport as the leader of the fleet. He was a highly competent and experienced seaman who had navigated the western waters, and was a man of sound sense, courage and character.

It was exceedingly good fortune, too, that Captain John Smith had offered his services to the Company in this venture, for no man among those who sailed was so well fitted for the wilderness struggle as he. He was only twenty-five at the time, but he had already spent a decade of his life as an adventurer and soldier in many lands. He had fought the Turks, been captured and made a slave, and had finally escaped to England. John Smith was setting forth on another adventure in high spirits, but it was the adventure itself and not gold that was the lure.

Just before sailing, Captain Newport was given a sealed box by the governing Council of the London Company. In it were the names of the men who would serve the colony as the first resident council, one of whom would be chosen president by the members themselves. The Captain was given strict instructions not to open the box before landing in Virginia.

And on December 20, 1606, everything being at last in readiness, the little fleet dropped down the Thames River from Blackwall. But they didn't sail far. The winds contrarily turned against them, and for six weeks they lay anchored in the channel near Dover.

But a fair-sailing day did finally come, and with a strong, favorable wind blowing, Captain Newport set the course southwestward for the Azores and sailed out of English waters. It was a long route, this course by way of the West Indies, but he wanted to take advantage of the trade winds. They reached the Azores and sailed on southeastward to the Canaries where fresh water was taken on, and then the prows of the little ships were pointed westward for the long voyage across the Atlantic.

It was on this tedious, sometimes storm-racked, stretch that Captain John Smith and Edward Wingfield became involved in an ugly quarrel. Wingfield was a merchant-adventurer, one of the patentees of the London Company who was coming over with the colonists.

Captain John Ratcliffe, seeking personal advantage perhaps, was quick to take Wingfield's part in the argument and incite the others against Captain Smith by spreading the rumor that he was conspiring to stage a mutiny. Whether this and other charges were true or not has never been proved. If Captain Ratcliffe had had his way, Smith would have swung from the gallows when they reached the West Indies. But Newport, in his position of authority, saved the Captain from this fate. Smith was bound in irons, however, and held a chained prisoner until they reached Virginia.

On March 24, 1607, the venturers reached Dominica, one of the islands of the West Indies. How fair the island—how sweet the smells of the green, flowering trees and bushes! It was inhabited by Indians who, the Englishmen learned, were cannibals and used poisoned arrowheads made of fish bones. But the savages showed only kindness to their visitors. They brought them gifts of pineapples, potatoes, plantons, tobacco and other fruits. In return, the voyagers gave the Indians copper jewels which they promptly tried to attach to their ears, noses and lips.

Safe aboard ship again, there was excitement for the men in a sea-fight which they watched from the decks. A whale was chased by a thresher and a swordfish, overtaken, and for two hours the fight raged in splashing waters. Finally the great sea-mammal was brought to an end by the sword thrusts and the flailings of the smaller but more agile fish.

Refreshed by their visit on Dominica, the voyagers weighed anchor and sailed on to Guadeloupe. They went ashore and found a bubbling hot spring in which Captain Newport boiled a piece of pork done in half an hour! A few days later they anchored at the island of Nevis. Everybody disembarked, and about a mile inland they came upon a clear stream and—took a bath. The ruffs and the fancy waistcoats and the doublets and trousers and stockings were hung on the bushes while they splashed in the cool water and cleansed their bodies after so many weeks since the last bath! There was a week's stay of recuperation here with plenty of game and fish to keep them well-fed.

On the island of Mona their casks were filled with fresh water and here they killed two wild boars and "feasted daily on a loathesome beast like a crocodile." The "loathesome beast" was an iguana which they described as being somewhat like a serpent, speckled on its belly like a toad. But they were glad to leave this spot for it was so hot that many of the men fainted. On the isle of Monica they replenished their larders with a great supply of wild game and birds' eggs, and on April 10th sailed from the West Indies where for three weeks they had found refreshing relaxation.

CHAPTER III   *The Colonists Choose
a Location*

AND NOW at long last the three little ships rocked gently at anchor on the west coast of Cape Henry. That first day on the shores of Virginia the colonists got acquainted with the natives. It was the kind of meeting that taught them the wisdom of always having a musket in hand even when stepping out for a leisurely walk in the woods. A party of some twenty-odd men went ashore to stretch and limber up and take a look-around. Nothing happened. They breathed deeply of the clean, sweet air of early spring, drank the cool water at crystal-clear springs and noted with satisfaction the green luxuriance of the new land and the great trees—pine,

[31]

walnut and oak—that grew almost to the water's edge.

Then at twilight on their way back to the ships one of the men suddenly cried out, "Look! Look yonder!" He pointed, and they saw a strange, terrifying sight. Creeping toward them from the hills on all fours, like bears, were many savages with bows carried between clenched teeth. Seeing themselves discovered, the "bears" suddenly rose up and let go a flight of arrows. One pierced Captain Gabriel Archer's hand, and a sailor was badly wounded by another. The answering volley of musket shot sent the savages scurrying into the woods and that was the last the men saw of them.

The incident was probably forgotten—by all except Captain Archer and the wounded sailor—that evening in the excitement of opening the sealed box that had been entrusted to Captain Newport's care. With what eager interest the men must have watched the Captain as he broke the seal and took out the important paper on which were written the names of those who were to be their governing council! Bartholomew Gosnold, Edward Wingfield, Christopher Newport, John Ratcliffe, John Martin, George Kendall and—John Smith! Consternation among those who had been his accusers —and his fellow-councilors promptly excluded him, for that was one of their privileges. But they released him from his shackles. Edward Wingfield was elected President, but it was an honor without prerogatives. His only function was to preside at the meetings and cast a double vote in case of a tie. Perhaps John Smith grunted his satisfaction over this!

The following day the shallop, which had been

brought over in sections, was put together and a selected group of "gentlemen" and soldiers set out in the small boat to navigate and explore their surroundings. The Indians, for a time, were happily absent from the scene. But almost everywhere they went they found traces of them. Roasted oysters they had left in one place the men ate with relish—very large and very delicate in taste, they said. An empty canoe made out of a whole tree and forty-five feet long. Grass recently burned and still smoking.

Toward the end of the day they began taking soundings of the near-by waters. Shallow in most places, but at a point of land northwest of Cape Henry they sounded to a depth of twelve fathoms and, because this gave them "good comfort," they named it Cape Comfort (Point Comfort).

On the last day of the month the ships sailed over to Cape Comfort and anchored there on its southern shore at the mouth of the James River. Again the shallop was manned and further explorations made. They were in populous Indian country now but the savages were friendly, and no doubt as curious as they. Redskin meeting Paleface made a great and elaborate show of courtesy and friendship. The hand on the heart was a sign of no bad intentions; and with this kind of introduction on the part of the palefaces, the savages of Kecoughtan were delighted to escort the strangers to their town.

A typical Indian "town" in Virginia in 1607 was located near a river or fresh spring. The houses were shaped like an arbor, or a kind of elongated Eskimo igloo. Supple branches from small trees were bent over and tied securely, then covered closely with mats or the bark of trees. Such dwellings were surprisingly weathertight—but smoky. In typical Indian fashion, there was a hole in the mid-top of the house for the escape of smoke from the central fire inside.

In Kecoughtan—"great town" in their language—the savages expressed their pleasure upon the arrival of the visitors from England by making a most doleful noise, prostrating themselves on the ground and clawing at the earth. The welcoming ceremony over, mats were brought out on which the guests were seated and then feasted. After that they smoked pipes—like the English ones, only bigger and with the bowl banded with copper. A weird dance followed that the English little understood. To them it was nothing but much shouting, howling and stamping on the ground, like noises made by devils or wolves. But they were grateful for the good will of the Indians, and at the conclusion of the ceremonies Captain Newport gave them the bright-colored beads and copper ornaments they prized so highly.

Similarly the Englishmen were entertained and made welcome by the Paspaheghs on the north side of the James River where an old chieftain made a long oration, no word of which they understood! Then the werowance of the Rappahannocks, who lived on the south side of the James near the Paspaheghs, sent a messenger bidding them to come and visit him. The word "werowance" among the Virginia Indians was the same as the word "sachem" in New England and meant leader, or chief.

The werowance of the Rappahannocks came down

himself to the waterside with his flute-players to welcome them. The Englishmen must have gaped before
they stepped ashore, for the chieftain's naked body was
painted crimson, his face blue, and he was adorned with
a spectacular assortment of feathers, birds, claws, copper jewels and pearl bracelets. For all that, they reported he entertained them with proud dignity and
that there was no laughter or unseemly behavior among
his followers.

After some days, all three ships entered the James
and sailed as far up the river as the Appomattox country, and on that upstream voyage passed what was to
become the site of their settlement. On the way downstream they again sailed by this site and then stopped
for a while at a point on the north bank which Captain
Archer favored for their location. Most of the colonists
approved this choice, but the mariners were against it
because of shoal waters near the bank. So again they
sailed upstream and made their choice of the spot they
had twice passed—a peninsula on the north side of the
river about thirty miles above Cape Comfort. They
overlooked some unfavorable features of the location,
or did not bother to explore them, because the water
was so deep close to the shore they could sail right up
to the bank and throw out a rope to secure their ships
to the trees that grew near the water's edge.

So here the fateful landing was made.

CHAPTER IV   *Indians Attack the Settlement*

WITH FANFARE OF TRUMPETS the colonists disembarked early on the morning of May 14th upon the historic spot that was to be their new home. The Reverend Robert Hunt offered up a prayer, and then the men went to work unloading their supplies and rigging up the tents in which they would live until more substantial shelters could be built. The first permanent English settlement in America began that day in the wilderness of Virginia. James Fort, the settlers called it at first, but soon the name was changed to Jamestown.

Not all could find lodging that first day and many had to spend another night aboard ship. The next morning all were up early to chop down the trees. As the clearings widened more tents were set up. Some of the men dug holes for shelter, like the dug-outs of the pioneers who settled on the western plains more than two hundred years later. Others fashioned rude sleeping quarters from the boughs of trees.

And that night the waves of the James lapped the sides of the three little ships that rode at anchor, the stars gleamed in the high heavens, and the men slept huddled together in their tents, dug-outs and under the tree boughs there in the swamps. Perhaps some of them looked up to the stars hopefully before they fell asleep, for only the stars seemed friendly in that lonely setting. The great ocean they had crossed lay to the east, separating them by three thousand miles from their homeland. Their nearest Christian neighbors were the hostile Spaniards, hundreds of miles south of them in Saint Augustine, Florida. A vast, uncharted wilderness stretched northward to the Pole. And to the west, where they expected to find a short water-passage leading to the Pacific Ocean and the Indies, were three thousand miles of desert and plains and mountain range. There was danger, as well as loneliness, all around them. For by day and by night, the Indians, hiding in the tall grasses, spied upon them, taking the measure of their strength and resistance.

There was no time, fortunately, to brood over the loneliness, and for a while the Jamestown campers were not molested by the savages. No man was more energetic than Captain George Kendall, who soon had a group busily at work building the first fort—nothing more than the great boughs and branches of trees fashioned together in the form of a half-moon, but it served for a time.

Something had to be sent back in the ships, so a few

of the settlers went to work cutting down trees which they sawed into clapboards. In England clapboards were oak boards of a certain size and thickness that were used for wainscoting and for making barrel staves. Getting that first cargo ready for the merchant-adventurers was back-breaking, hand-blistering work, and the men soon began to feel the weakening effects of the hot, steamy climate.

No man could afford to be idle though, and during those first few weeks there were no shirkers. Even the "gentlemen" fell to with a will and did their share. They made clearings and prepared the ground for the first gardens. Some busied themselves making nets for the fishermen. And others got ready a rude church where they would worship until a better one could be built. An old sail was hung between two trees and in front of it a plank on two supports served as an altar. For seats there were tree-trunks stripped of their branches and laid in rows upon the ground. There was no roof. It was under the blue heavens that the weary men worshipped that first Sunday at the services of the Church of England conducted by the Reverend Robert Hunt. And with the fragrance and the flowering loveliness of dogwood and redbud and honeysuckle all about them, they must have felt very close to God—and a little less lonely.

In the midst of these activities, the werowance of the Paspaheghs, Wochinchopunck, came to call on the pale-faces who had settled in his domain. He came attended by one hundred armed savages. The colonists were armed, too, when they turned out to greet their visitors. By sign-language the werowance urged them to lay aside their arms, and assured them that he would give them all the land they wanted.

Presently the redskins were swarming all over the place and a watchful, wary colonist spied one of them in the act of stealing a hatchet. There was a brief exchange of blows that might have led to serious trouble. But the werowance suddenly called his painted warriors together and they departed in high dudgeon. The harassed colonists came rightly to the conclusion that day that "these savages are naturally great thieves."

Not all the men were on the island at this time felling trees and getting the little settlement started. Captain Newport had decided that he should make at least one voyage of exploration up the river before his return to England. Somewhere beyond its upper reaches they might find that mythical waterway to the Indies for which explorers had been hopefully searching since Columbus's time. Newport had chosen Captain John Smith as his companion-in-command, proving his high regard for the man who would have been hanged if some of the others had had their way, and with a party of twenty men they had set out from Jamestown one fine morning in their shallop headed up-river.

The party passed many small Indian habitations along the way, and on the sixth day found further passage blocked by rocks and falls. They had reached, as they thought, the head of the James River, and on May 24th they set up a cross at this spot and proclaimed

"James, King of England, to have the most right to it."
But it was not the short-water-cut they had hoped to
find to the spice islands.

Here on the site where the city of Richmond stands
today was a mean little Indian village called Powhatan.
Twelve small houses sat on a hill in the midst of flourishing cornfields. It was one of many such towns ruled
by the great chief also called Powhatan. No doubt the
colonists had their eyes on the ripening ears of corn
when they went ashore to pay the Powhatans a visit.
They were received with friendliness, presents were
exchanged, and the Indians promised to come to the
fort soon.

Other towns were visited and some trading was done.
Newport was good at it, and Smith would soon prove
to be the best man of them all at this game of barter. It
may have been on this trip that Captain Newport found
a sizeable quantity of ore which he took back to England with the hope that it would make the eyes of the
adventurers of the London Company pop.

Shocking news awaited the explorers upon their
return to the fort a few days later. The Indians had
attacked! They had lain in the high, shielding grasses
and reeds and thickets, watching the toiling settlers day
after day. They had seen little groups go out to the
garden patches with their tools and lay aside their arms.
They had watched others hacking away at the tough
cypresses after stacking their muskets against near-by
trees. They had seen stragglers coming back from fishing down the river.

And one day they had closed in on the unsuspecting

workers, about two hundred of them with their werowance, Wochinchopunck, and let fly their deadly arrows. A young boy fell dead. Eleven settlers were wounded. Among the more prominent men in the colony, Gosnold, Ratcliffe, Martin and Kendall suffered injuries. And President Wingfield had the hair-raising experience of seeing an arrow go whizzing through his beard!

For some weeks the poorly fortified fort was besieged by the skulking Indians ready to shoot any settler who dared to venture outside alone. Eustace Clovell was one who paid with his life for recklessly taking leave of the guard. With six arrows sticking in his body, he staggered into the fort one day crying, "Arm! Arm!" Eight days later he was dead.

Some of the men felt very bitter toward the President of the Council. They may have wished that the arrow had pierced more than his beard. For he had not taken the proper steps to defend them, they charged. A more substantial fort should already have been built, and the men should have been trained in defense drill.

There were two fortunate outcomes of the savages' attacks. A friendly Indian took the trouble to come and tell them that it would be a good idea to cut down the tall grasses that screened their lurking enemies. Belatedly they did. Then everybody set to work building the fort that would really be an adequate means of protection and defense.

It was to be a palisaded fort with long stakes or small tree trunks driven deep into the ground. On about half an acre of level ground they dug a moat, or trench, in the shape of a triangle, and above this erected the stout fourteen-foot walls of the palisade. The south side of the fort, about one hundred forty yards long, in which the main gate had been cut, faced the river front. The east and west sides were one hundred yards in length, and at each angle of the triangle watch-towers, called bulwarks, were built in the shape of a half-moon and cannon mounted upon them.

For a time the town itself would be inside the fort. Within the palisaded walls were rows of houses which followed the triangular outline of the fort. And in the middle were such buildings as the market place, the guard house, a chapel and storehouses for provisions and ammunition.

The building method which they brought over and followed was that which was common in England during the fourteenth and fifteenth centuries. Their early houses in Jamestown were not log structures, but buildings which made use of crotches, or forks, to support the roof and the walls of upright timbers. After the framework had been laid, the roofs were thatched with sedge or rushes and plastered with clay.

By the middle of June the fort was finished and all was in readiness for the improved accommodation and protection of the colonists who had toiled for six long, hot weeks. The ships had been loaded with a heavy cargo of clapboards, sassafras roots and some samples of mineral earth. Captain Newport felt he could now safely leave the struggling little group and return to England to report on the progress they had made.

In command of the *Sarah Constant* and the *Good-*

speed, the pinnace having been left for the use of the colonists, the Captain turned eastward on June 22, 1607, and sailed down the James. He arrived at Plymouth Harbor in England on July 29, 1607, and that same day sent to the Earl of Salisbury, Secretary of State for England and Lord Treasurer, a glowing report on the steaming little settlement he had left five weeks earlier. The colony had been successfully planted in Virginia. The colonists had explored the country for some two hundred miles and found it excellent and very rich in gold and copper. Some of the gold-ore had been brought for assay and it would soon be shown to his Lordship, to his Majesty and to the rest of the Lords.

The report that had been sent by the local council in Virginia, and which Captain Newport would deliver to the Superior Council in England, was not quite so optimistic. They had to explain that cargo of clapboards. And they had to let the Council know what their plight and their need was. But they could not afford to paint too dark a picture for fear the adventurers of the Company would lose faith and hope in their colonizing efforts. So they apologized for the clapboards and pleaded for additional supplies. Then, by way of stirring both hope and action, they added that if the necessary supplies did not come the all-devouring Spaniards might appear and lay their greedy hands upon the gold-showing mountains in Virginia!

CHAPTER V   *John Smith Escapes Death*

BUT THE MEN back in swampy Jamestown were not thinking of gold and clapboards while the lords and merchant-adventurers in England were reading about the excellent country of Virginia that was so rich in gold and copper. They were thinking of nothing but—food.

The larder at James Fort was almost as empty as old Mother Hubbard's cupboard when Captain Newport left late in June, 1607. He had thought there was enough to keep the wolf from the gate of the little palisaded fort until his return with a shipload of supplies, but six months passed before he sailed up the James

[44]

again. And during that time there was terrible suffering and death at Jamestown.

There had been little enough to unload from the ships when they landed and started their settlement. The long voyage and the weeks spent in the Bay while they were looking for a site on which to locate had greatly reduced their precious food stores. The gardens were planted late, and as the days became hotter and more humid, the men, who were not used to planting and ploughing in the first place, neglected to tend them.

While the ships were there, the colonists improved their daily rations by bartering with the sailors. For the sailors, who had to be fit for the return voyage, fared better than they. A supply of biscuits had been kept for them and they were soon pilfering biscuits from under the cook's nose to trade for one thing and another with the hungry settlers. After the seamen departed there was nothing left except the "common kettle."

Out of the common kettle each man was given once a day, by strict order of President Wingfield, a half pint of wheat mixed with the same amount of barley, and nobody knew how many weevils! This frugal, nauseous mixture was boiled in water that came from the river, which was also the source of their drinking water. At the flood it was very salty, and at low tide brackish and full of slime and filth.

Not only were the men half-starved, but their living conditions were almost unbearable. The tents had rotted away and the crowded cabins inside the little palisaded fort were insufferably hot and unsanitary.

Ill-fed and ill-housed as these pioneers were, the work had to go on and they had to keep watch by day and by night for fear of Indian attacks.

So it was that in the sticky, humid days of early summer the unfortunate wretches began to sicken and die. They were stricken with such cruel diseases as burning fevers, dysentery, malaria, strange swellings—and some died so suddenly that nobody knew what had mercifully taken them off so quickly. Many, it seemed, simply died of starvation.

By August they were taking leave of this world at such a rate, sometimes three and four in a night, that the living could not decently take care of the dead. In the early morning before the hot sun rose, the bodies would be dragged out of the cabins like dogs to be buried. And with the sun, that would add to their wretchedness, rose the groans and pitiful outcries of those who lay suffering without relief on hot pallets and beds in the close quarters of the fort. Everywhere there was misery and death at Jamestown. And on August 22nd Captain Bartholomew Gosnold, member of the council and one of the colony's most useful and inspiring leaders, died.

With the life of the little settlement itself hanging by a thread, it was a time when those who were able to stand should have stood together in harmony and unity of purpose. But even at such a time as this, during that fateful summer of 1607, in the midst of suffering and death, there was no end of petty quarreling and bickering among the leaders.

At the very outset there were mutterings and grumblings against Edward Wingfield who, as President of the council, had never been popular. Captain Smith, who had been ill and had recovered, charged that Wingfield had suffered neither want nor sickness because he had helped himself to the provisions and had even kept a liberal supply of brandy for his own use. So President Wingfield was put out of office by the other councilors and Captain John Ratcliffe appointed to take his place. Captain Kendall suffered the same disgrace as Wingfield for some misdemeanor, and, on the first of December, was condemned by a jury and shot to death for his alleged leadership in a conspiracy to board the *Discovery* and escape to England.

During these grim times either the Spaniards or the Indians might easily have stepped in and put a quick end to what already looked like a dying colony. The Spanish ambassador in London had reported Newport's arrival from Virginia and his plans to return, and was urging his sovereign, King Philip III, to hang every English villain in Jamestown. But Philip was slow to act, and somehow some of the "villains" managed to survive. This was mainly, or entirely, due to the generosity of the Indians who might also easily have wiped out the few weak survivors at this time. Instead they took pity on them and came, just when even the wormy wheat and barley were almost gone, bearing gifts of corn, ready-made bread, fruits and other provisions.

The thirty-eight weak survivors feasted, rejoiced and took heart after the ghastly experiences of the summer. Cooler weather had come and with it the fowls to the river—swans, geese, ducks and cranes. Captain John

Ratcliffe had been a poor choice for President, but there weren't many to choose from, and Captain John Smith, who hated him, took matters more or less into his own hands and nobody objected.

Always impatient with weakness in men, the energetic Captain Smith forgot the harrowing ordeal the colonists had been through and complained that most of them would rather starve and rot in idleness than do anything for their own good. He set an example by his own industry, and soon had them binding thatch, building new houses, repairing the palisades and generally restoring the settlement to order. When the corn and other provisions the savages had brought were depleted and they did not return, he decided the time had come when the salvation of the settlement depended upon successful trading with the natives. No man was so well fitted for this undertaking as Captain John Smith himself, and Captain Smith knew it! So now he got ready to set forth to trade with the Indians.

The little Indian town of Kecoughtan on Point Comfort down at the mouth of the James was the first place visited in the shallop. And here Smith traded successfully for fish, oysters, bread, venison and sixteen bushels of corn. On the way back to the fort he increased his store of corn to thirty bushels by shrewd bargaining with the Warraskoyacks. But this was still a scant supply for the winter ahead. So, after the Captain and his men had feasted on the good bread, the Virginia pease, the pumpkins and the persimmons that were now plentiful, they pushed off in the shallop for more trading.

During the next few weeks, while the November

days grew shorter and chillier, they ranged up-river in Chickahominy country. The Chickahominy River flows into the James a few miles above Jamestown and the name means "coarse-pounded corn people" or "hominy people."

It was very evident that the Chickahominies were "corn people." Their country was a corn-trader's paradise! Smith made the most of his opportunities. Manosquosick, Oraniocke, Mansa,—corn in plenty in all the towns he stopped at, and the Chickahominies eager to trade!

Smith knew the tricks of trading by now. "I showed them the copper and the hatchets they should have for corn," he said, and shrewdly added, "and what I liked I bought, but lest they should see how great was my want, I went higher up the river."

And then they came to Mamanahunt. "There were two hundred people assembled with such abundance of corn I loaded our shallop and could have loaded a ship," the jubilant Captain told the settlers, while they were carrying the corn ashore after his return. One more trip he made to this best of all the corn-towns and returned again in the old shallop that groaned and squeaked under a load of corn heavy enough to sink it!

That was enough corn-trading for a while. There was no threat now of starvation and Captain John Smith had other business to attend to. The London adventurers were expecting him to do some more exploring, particularly up the Chickahominy to the falls—there was still the teasing promise, or hope, of a passage to the South Sea.

The shallop moved slowly up the river again, and Captain Smith's keen, observant eyes missed nothing, as usual, along the way. The great plenty of swans, cranes, geese, ducks and mallards on the river—wide sweep of down-ward curving wings; still, white forms resting on stilts; little gray huddles that came to life with a sudden swoop and splash into the gray waters—everywhere the wild beauty of wild life. Landward, there was the ever-changing scene of marshes, hills and valleys, Indian habitations and fertile cornfields.

The explorers came to a point, finally, high up-river where the stream narrowed and the current was swift. There was danger to the cumbersome craft, so Captain Smith stopped at an Indian village along the shore where he hired a canoe and two Indian guides. Seven men were left in the shallop while Smith and two of his company, along with the guides, continued twenty miles farther up the river.

After having eaten a boiled dinner on the river bank, the Captain set off with one of his Indian guides to do a little exploring of the wild terrain on foot. The two men left there with the other guide—Thomas Emry and John Robinson—were instructed to have their muskets ready to fire at sight of an Indian.

Within the hour Captain Smith was startled by a sudden outburst of savage yells, though he had heard no warning shot from his men. Suspecting betrayal on the part of the guides, he seized his Indian companion and bound his arms. But the savage was as ignorant as Smith of what was happening and urged him to flee.

At that moment the Captain's right thigh was grazed by an arrow, and the next he was defending himself with his pistol and his guide, whom he used as a shield against the yelling demons who came swarming out of the woods with their bows raised and their arrows flying. The attack ended as suddenly as it had begun, and Smith, miraculously alive and not seriously injured, found himself surrounded by two hundred braves of the Pamunkey tribe of whom Opechancanough, brother of the great Powhatan, was chief.

The Indian guide was loyal. He explained that the Captain was on a peaceful mission and pleaded that he be permitted to return to his boat. The Pamunkey savages replied that the men in the boat had been slain and demanded Smith's arms. This misadventure had occurred in a swamp, and in the midst of the parleying Smith, who was still circling about brandishing his pistol, suddenly sank down and stuck fast in a quagmire with his Indian beside him. Maybe it had required a bog for two hundred savages to lay hold of the doughty Captain. Anyway, even he now realized that further resistance was useless and cast aside his arms. He was unceremoniously pulled out and led before the Chief.

The resourceful Captain was equal to the occasion, for he was also armed with a compass, and he rightly guessed that this little gadget would tickle the fancy and excite the curiosity of the savage chieftain whose only compass had been the stars. Opechancanough leaned forward as eagerly as a child and watched the needle swing from one direction to another. Then he was permitted to hold the compass and lo, the little needle behaved for him as it had for the paleface Captain. Sheer magic, and the chief was enchanted!

Having already mastered some of the Indian tongues, and with the aid of sign-language, Smith now began to talk for time. He explained the use of the compass and told the ignorant savage, as best he could, about the rotation of the earth, the eclipses of sun and moon and the course of the stars and the planets—and "how the sun did chase the night around the world continually."

Finally Opechancanough interrupted to do some talking himself. He made what Smith thought, under the circumstances, was a kind speech and then fed him. But he was in no mood to release his prisoner, who was now conducted to where the canoe was anchored. Thomas Emry was nowhere about, but there lay Master John Robinson slain, with twenty or thirty arrows sticking in him. A grim sight, and as they marched on, Smith expected to be executed at each place where they stopped. But Opechancanough knew this was no ordinary paleskin who, by chance, had become his captive. It was for him a triumphal tour, a kind of Roman holiday. Captain John Smith was exhibited all over the Tidewater country, and in the Indian villages the women and children flocked out of their mat-covered, arbor-like houses to see him. There was feasting and dancing and a good time for everybody except the apprehensive prisoner.

Nothing came of a letter that Smith was permitted to write and send by Indian messenger to Jamestown. He had explained to Opechancanough that he wanted to let the colonists know he was being kindly treated so they would not take revenge on him.

There were more conversations in the intervals between marching. Smith tried to intimidate his captor by impressing him with the power of the white man. He told how well armed they were at Jamestown, of their great ships that sailed the high seas, and warned that if any harm befell him Captain Christopher Newport would surely take revenge upon his return. The Chief seemed interested in hearing all this and about the Christian God, but Smith continued to be well fed, well cared for, and—well guarded.

At last Opechancanough wearied of marching and exhibiting his captive and sent him by armed escort to his brother, Powhatan. Powhatan, the great King, or Emperor, was ruler of numerous tribal groups held loosely together in a union called the "confederacy." The capital of his confederacy on the north side of the York River, where he lived, was the town of Werowocomoco, which means "the house of the werowance."

And here, in Werowocomoco, Captain John Smith met the Emperor Powhatan in one of the arbor-like houses. It was a case of great Redman meeting great Paleface, for both were great leaders and equally shrewd and crafty. But John Smith was a young man and Powhatan was growing old. His black hair was graying and he had a dour look, but he was still tall and straight and well-proportioned, and his mind was keen.

The Emperor received Captain Smith, not from a lofty throne, but from a great mat-covered bed, a foot high, on which he reclined covered with raccoon skins and wearing many chains of white beads around his neck. An Indian woman sat at his head and another at his feet. Ranged on each side were his chief men sitting on mats, and behind them young women of the tribe resplendent in red paint and with heavy chains of beads over their shoulders.

There is the story John Smith first told of his kindly welcome by the dour-faced old Emperor and of the long conversations they had before he was sent back to Jamestown.

"The cause of your coming—why did you come to our shores?" Powhatan wanted to know.

And Smith, nimbly making up his explanations as he went along, replied, "It was the Spaniards. We were in a fight with our enemy, the Spaniards. They had overpowered us and we were forced to retreat."

The Emperor was listening attentively but Smith could only guess what he was thinking as he continued, "Then we were caught in a terrible storm that drove us into Chesapeake Bay where our pinnace began to leak. We were forced to stay there to mend it and await the coming of Captain Christopher Newport, my father."

Smith always referred to Newport as his father in his conversations with Powhatan. When the Emperor wanted to know why they had then gone up the James in their boats, Smith was ready with a sly answer. He wanted to draw out Powhatan on the subject of what lay beyond the falls, so he said, "Beyond the river where there is salt water are a people called the Monacans who killed a child of my father, Captain Newport, and whose death we wanted to revenge."

The old Emperor was a good story-teller, too. He had Smith leaning forward, agog with interest, as he told of mythical kingdoms beyond the falls where mighty nations lived upon the shores of a great sea, and beyond them a people who wore short coats and passed that way in ships like those of the English. Perhaps Powhatan learned that day that this trick of assuring the English that everything they hoped to find was there beyond the falls would be very useful to him in his dealings with them.

Then there was the story Smith told years later of how the lovely, little Pocahontas, favorite child of the old Emperor, saved his life.

According to this story, Powhatan had not received him with kind words of welcome. He had promptly ordered his execution and the Captain was led with hands bound behind him to a great stone.

Several strapping, painted braves had come forward with heavy clubs and the prisoner had been forced upon his knees before the block. He had made his last plea to no avail and his head had been laid upon the stone. But just as the clubs were raised to bash out his brains, there was the sudden flash of a lithe, bronze body and Smith's head was being cradled in the arms of the child who had rushed forward at the risk of her own life to save him.

Pocahontas, a mere child of twelve or thirteen years of age, had raised pleading brown eyes to her old father and begged for the life of the prisoner. Not only was she dearer to him than any other, but it was a custom among the Indians to permit a woman to claim the life of a captive. So Powhatan had relented and Captain

John Smith's life was spared. That, according to this version of the story, was the beginning of the lasting friendship between the English Captain and the gentle Indian girl who played so important a part in the life of Jamestown thereafter.

Whichever story is true, Captain John Smith arrived safely back in Jamestown on January 2, 1608. To the astonished settlers it was almost as if he had come back from the grave for they had given up hope of ever seeing him again, certain that he had been killed by the Indians.

And on the evening of that same day, Captain Christopher Newport anchored with the first supply. It was a day of high excitement and great rejoicing for the men there in Jamestown who had known too little of good fortune in their wilderness settlement.

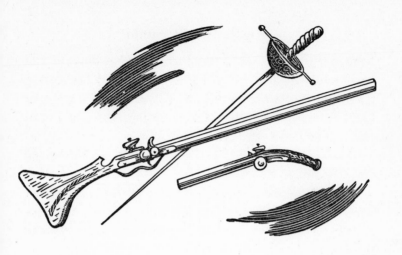

CHAPTER VI *Christopher Newport Meets Powhatan*

THERE WAS WARMTH and good cheer inside the palisaded walls of the little fort that cold January evening of the day of Captain John Smith's return from captivity and Captain Christopher Newport's arrival with the first supply. The little group of dispirited men who had survived the horrors of the past summer were now struggling to keep alive in the bitter cold of an unusually severe winter, and this day's blessings brought a glow to their haggard faces and a lift to their drooping spirits. They crowded together around the great warming blaze of an open fire and listened eagerly to the tales and the news that the two captains vied in telling.

There were newcomers among them now, colonists who had come over in the supply ship to fill their dwindling ranks, and one who had been sent by the Council in England to take his place as a member of their local council. Perhaps Master Matthew Scrivener and Captain John Smith knew when they shook hands that night that they would become good friends—a wise and understanding man, the Captain, who got along well with so few of the leaders, later described him.

"But these are not all the men who set out to join you," Captain Newport said after he had introduced them. "There was the *Phoenix*, another tall ship commanded by Captain Nelson, that sailed with us. She, too, carried settlers and supplies. But the *Phoenix* was badly damaged during a storm and is now in some West Indian harbor being repaired. No doubt Captain Nelson will come sailing up our river soon."

The old settlers, those of the first-comers who were left, raised a great shout at this good news and lifted mugs of foaming beer that had been brought ashore that very evening from the ship. They drank to the jovial mariners who were in their midst, assuring them there were no limits to the trading they could do on this visit to Jamestown.

The night wore on and the men became groggy from all the excitement and the warmth and the beer. Some of the newcomers, weary from the long voyage, had already rolled over on the floor and gone to sleep. Before the rest separated, Captain Nelson said, "Tomorrow we'll unload the stores of beef, pork, oil, butter, cheeses and such like, and the tools and materials we've brought."

And Captain Smith added, "And the corn our friend

Powhatan sent with me." The Captain never came back, not even from captivity, without the corn that he knew was so essential to the life of the settlers.

Just a few days later gloom settled upon the fort again, this time in a pall of smoke. Jamestown had its first fire in the dead of that bitter winter.

Some said it was the newcomers who, by their carelessness, had accidentally started the conflagration. Nobody knew. The blaze began in one of the buildings outside the fort and soon the flames were leaping across the thatched roofs and consuming the houses, the huts and the shacks as if they had been so many corn-shocks. The palisaded fort, some ten or twelve yards distant, caught fire and burned like tinder. And the men could only stand there shaking in the biting cold and helplessly watch the buildings on which they had toiled so hard during the spring and summer go up in smoke.

Nor was that all the loss. Clothing, bedding, weapons and precious food stores were quickly consumed. The Reverend Hunt lost his entire library and everything else he possessed except the clothes on his back. But no one heard a word of complaint from him. And certainly there was no bemoaning from Captain John Smith. But even the complainers were a heroic lot as they again made shift as best they could, throwing together whatever was at hand for shelter. It was scant protection from the cold and there were more deaths during the weeks that followed. With the coming of spring and mild weather, new buildings would go up—meanwhile there was suffering.

Meanwhile, too, there was the immediate problem of

getting some kind of cargo ready for Captain Newport to take back to the adventurers on his second return trip to England. The adventurers had invested a great deal of money in the colony and as yet they had realized little, if anything, on their investment. Unless something could be found that would make this venture profitable to them they would risk no more money, and the struggling little colony would be yet another failure.

Lumber had not proved a satisfactory commodity because it took up too much cargo space for what its sale brought in English markets. The adventurers were still hopefully directing the efforts of the colonists toward finding a short route to the South Sea that would bring closer the rich spice and silk trade of the Far East, and toward the discovery of valuable mineral deposits.

Then, while Newport waited early in 1608 for something to carry back in his ship, the gold fever broke out among the colonists and they went crazily prospecting in those gold-showing mountains. John Smith, who was all for loading the ship with lumber, was disgusted and went off with Newport for a visit with Powhatan.

Before he left he tried to tell the settlers just how crazy they were. He strode angrily up and down the council hall arguing heatedly that it was the worst mischief they had yet got into. "Nothing," he shouted at them, and particularly at Councilor Captain John Martin, "has ever tormented me more than to see our necessary business neglected just to freight this drunken ship with so much gilded dirt."

The Captain knew it would take many weeks, as

indeed it did, to fill the ship with the gilded dirt, and that rankled. "There's little need and less reason," he cried, "for the ship to stay tied up here for weeks with the mariners' wages running high and our victuals running low."

But the gold fever had to run its course. It was some time before it subsided. It was some time before the Captain's anger subsided, too. Afterward he summed up the whole crazy business by scornfully saying, "There was no talk, no hope, no work, but dig gold, wash gold, refine gold, load gold."

Up on the York River at Werowocomoco, not many miles from Jamestown, the old Emperor was pondering his own problems. He not only had his loosely organized and scattered tribes to think about and hold together, but the coming of the white men to Indian lands had presented a wholly new problem that had to be dealt with. Powhatan had quickly taken the measure of their strength in the weapons they brought with them, so different from, and so much more effective than, the Indians' bows and arrows. He wanted some of the palefaces' guns and swords and tools. Their weakness, he knew, was lack of food, and the Emperor had food in plenty to trade.

The Indians kept a watchful eye on the little settlement down on the James, so Powhatan knew their plight after the calamitous fire and he knew that the great father, Captain Christopher Newport, had arrived. He did not want his paleface friends to suffer hunger and he wanted even more to meet their chief, for thus Captain John Smith had described Newport.

So it was that the hunger of the unfortunate settlers was for a time appeased by Powhatan's bounty. His painted warriors came padding through the woods bearing great baskets of bread and heaped-up plenty of wild game and a fat deer slung over their shoulders. They came as messengers, too, urging Captain Smith to return for the corn their Emperor had ready for him and —would not the great white father come with him?

The great white father had also been thinking about the great Indian chief and was eager to meet him. It would be an advantage to the English to have so powerful a native ally who might also aid them in locating gold mines and finding that route to the South Sea. So, with time on his hands while the men dug for the gilded dirt, Captain Christopher Newport got ready for a visit to Powhatan with Captain John Smith.

The day came when both the shallop and the pinnace sailed down the James, the one commanded by Captain Smith and the other by Captain Newport. Master Scrivener was aboard as Smith's helper, and there were enough soldiers and sailors with them for any emergency. The boats rounded Point Comfort and headed up the York River for Werowocomoco.

Since Captain Smith was conducting Newport on his first formal visit to the red chieftain it was decided upon arrival that he should go ashore first to announce his coming. The Emperor's son, Nantaquaus, and a group of his chief men were on hand to welcome the visitors and escort them to his habitation. But the wary Captain Smith did not disembark unescorted. Twenty armed men, clad in thick leather coats, accompanied him, and he took the precaution of mingling them among the savages as they started off. "Most of their courage comes from fear of others," the experienced Captain had said time and again, and he didn't forget it even when he was paying them a friendly visit.

Coming into Powhatan's presence this time as a visitor rather than a captive, Captain John Smith was given a royal welcome. The proud old Chief, attired in a great robe of skins, smiled upon his paleface friend and invited him to sit upon the royal mat-covered bed, while the long room resounded with shouts of joy from his assembled attendants. Platters of bread and venison and beans were brought in and after the Captain and his men had feasted, three of the Emperor's chief men came forward to deliver orations.

Captain John Smith heard himself proclaimed a werowance, or chief, of Powhatan, and all the palefaces on the shores of the James declared to be not strangers or Paspaheghs but Powhatans. Always there would be friendship between them—a perpetual league of friendship.

The paleface Captain listened and smiled his pleasure as the speakers writhed and shouted their devotion, but he was saying to himself, "Yes, I'll believe in your friendship until you have convenient opportunity to betray us." But when the three orators finally retired, he rose and made a pretty speech himself in which he expressed his appreciation and assured them that the white man was the red man's friend.

The next day Captain Christopher Newport came ashore and, with much fanfare of trumpets blaring the

news of his coming, proceeded to Powhatan's dwelling
where the great white father and the great Indian chief
were formally introduced. Again there was shouting
and feasting and dancing and speech-making. And then
the three chiefs began the business of the visit—trading.
For four days they traded.

At the outset the old Emperor displayed his shrewd-
ness by scorning to trade as his subjects did. "Captain
Newport," he said, "it is not in keeping with my great-
ness to trade in a peddling manner for trifles. You know
I have respect for you as a great werowance. Therefore
show me all of your commodities. What I like I will
take and pay you according to what I think is their
value."

Smith, acting as interpreter, was quick to tell Newport that it was Powhatan's intention to cheat him. This
was an old trick he had learned in trading with the
Chickahominies. But Newport was eager to impress
Powhatan with his own power and prestige, and not
too much interested in how much corn he got in the
trade anyway. So he laid out everything—the hatchets,
the bells, the pins, the needles and the copper articles.
And he paid dearly for the corn he got in return.

Then Smith, who was both disgusted and angry with
Newport, took over. And now he brought out the
strings of blue beads that he had held back. The old
Chief's face lighted up when he saw those blue beads—
blue! The beads on his embroidered leather pillows
were white, and the heavy strands around the necks of
his bronze maidens were white. These were blue, and

Smith drove a hard bargain. For two pounds of blue beads he got two hundred bushels of corn!

Captain John Smith was the trader and he was practical enough to know the value of corn. Captain Christopher Newport was thinking about the silks and spices that could be shipped by that short route across the South Sea. Before he left Werowocomoco he had an important conference with Powhatan and his chief men at which a plan was discussed in detail for conquering their enemies the Monacans who occupied and ruled the country around and above the falls. Both the Monacans and the falls were barriers to the great Sea that Newport thought lay just beyond. Smith, skeptical of the venture, was certain that some treachery would be involved if they placed their faith and hopes in Powhatan. But the Emperor had no intention of carrying out the plans he had seriously discussed with Newport.

Before returning to the fort, the Englishmen went up the Pamunkey River to call on the king who had had such a good time parading Captain John Smith as a prisoner. This time the Captain came well armed and well guarded and the women and children came out, not to stare at him, but to pay their respects. Opechancanough entertained him and Master Scrivener and Captain Newport with much feasting and dancing, and more corn was stored on the shallop after the trading sessions at which Smith again bargained shrewdly and closely with the blue beads. They parted, as they had with Powhatan, with words and signs of love and friendship, and on March 9, 1608, the heavily loaded

[65]

pinnace and shallop tied up to the anchoring trees at Jamestown.

It was not until a month later, on April 10, that Newport's tall ship with its cargo of gilded dirt was ready to set sail for England. Contrary to the instructions of the Council in London, the white father had sent Emperor Powhatan a parting gift of twenty swords in token of good will and friendship, and Powhatan's parting gift to him was as many turkeys as five hefty warriors could bring to the ship. Captain Smith and Master Scrivener accompanied the departing ship in the shallop as far as Cape Henry and there waved farewell.

With the gilded dirt out of the way and the fever subsiding, they came back to the dilapidated little settlement and really went to work. The settlers hardly knew that the weak Captain John Ratcliffe was President of their council, for it was John Smith who now supervised all their activities. And there was Master Scrivener, too. "We divided the rebuilding of the town between us," said Smith generously, speaking of his right-hand man.

There was much to do. So many trees to fell for rebuilding the fort, the storehouse, the church and all the dwellings that were needed; and there was the spring sowing that could not be neglected.

The settlers were busily at work on April 20th hewing away at the tough trees and planting corn in the furrowed fields when a general alarm was sounded. "INDIANS!" Every man dropped his hoe, his saw, or his axe, grabbed his musket and raced for the settlement.

But they were halted by a panting messenger who shouted good news from afar: "A ship! A tall ship coming up the James!"

And standing there on the river bank, the panicky thought of Indians forgotten, they saw her—saw the *Phoenix* with fair sails spread to the gentle spring breeze, slowly plowing up the broad waters. After three months of delay in the West Indies, Captain Nelson had arrived with the rest of the new colonists and the supplies and provisions with which he had sailed from England with Captain Newport. All told, the two captains had now landed about one hundred new settlers, and among the men who stepped off the *Phoenix* were—builders! And six tailors, two goldsmiths, two refiners, two apothecaries, a gunsmith, a blacksmith, a cooper and a tobacco-pipe maker!

The men of Jamestown went back to their labors heartened by this good fortune which had so unexpectedly come to them. A new church went up, their second house of worship, and in a short time more substantial dwellings were standing there in the Virginia wilderness, better houses than had ever stood here before. They were roofed with the bark of trees, in imitation of the Indian dwellings, which gave greater protection from storms and the severities of winter weather, and kept the rooms cooler in summer. The builders were learning something even in this wild environment. There were big, wide chimneys, and delicately woven Indian mats gave the rooms their first touch of beauty.

While most of the men were at work in the fields or

on the new buildings, and some of them guarded the settlement, the council was wrangling over the old problem of what kind of cargo Captain Nelson should take back to England in the *Phoenix*. John Smith was now a member of this governing group, and so was Master John Scrivener. Together they argued angrily against Captain John Martin's plan to fill the ship with ore that had a glint of gold in it—some more of that gilded dirt. And this time Smith and Master Scrivener had their way. The *Phoenix* sailed on May 20th with a cargo of cedar.

John Martin left for England in the ship, too. Of the original seven members of the council, Captain Bartholomew Gosnold had died, Captain George Kendall had been shot, President Edward Wingfield had been returned to England a prisoner aboard Captain Newport's ship, and now Captain John Martin was leaving. Captain John Smith, who had arrived in chains and with the threat of execution hanging over him, had emerged the strongest and ablest leader among them. On September 10, 1608, he would become president of the council.

CHAPTER VII *John Smith Explores the Tide-Water Country*

ANOTHER SUMMER of soggy heat was beginning to sap the vitality of the Jamestown settlers and bring suffering and sickness and death again to many of them. But they had far more comfort and security this second summer on the swampy island than they had had the previous one. With adequate food supplies in the storehouse and the new bark-roofed dwellings completed, Captain John Smith felt they could weather the discomforts and diseases of the humid season and hold the little settlement together with none other than their president, Captain John Ratcliffe, to watch over them.

John Smith, who by the sheer force of his strong

personality had become their real leader, had other plans for the summer. The weather, no matter how humid, put no brake upon his driving energies and ambitions. And that summer of 1608 he planned to explore the great bay that lay to the east and through whose capes they had entered. The canny Indian trader would turn explorer and geographer of Chesapeake Bay which, in his own words, "till then was utterly unknown to any Christian."

No doubt the hardy, intrepid Captain had some difficulty recruiting the twelve men and Dr. Walter Russell who went with him in the shallop. About half of them were the "gentlemen" for whom he had so little respect and the rest were soldiers. Captain Smith had confidence in his soldiers, men of action like himself and toughened by hardships and dangers. He had even more confidence in his ability to handle any situation, no matter how difficult or unpromising.

On June 2nd of that summer of 1608 the shallop was on its way downstream headed for the bay that extended some two hundred miles from south to north and whose western and eastern shorelines were raggedly indented by innumerable rivers, creeks and inlets. On the first of his two expeditions during this summer, Captain John Smith crossed over to the Eastern Shore, after rounding Point Comfort, determined "to search every inlet and bay fit for harbors and habitations." The London adventurers were mainly interested in finding out whether this great body of water would give them access to the South Sea—Captain Smith wanted to know the geography of this part of the New

World and what resources could be found in the land.

It turned out to be a summer when wind, rain, thunder and lightning bedeviled and imperiled the explorers in the open boat. They suffered from lack of fresh water, too, and often fresh water was the main object of their search as the shallop sailed slowly northward past the many isles of the bay. Some they found inhabited by savages who were not always friendly—others were wild, uninhabited and desolate. A few days after their discovery of the Wicomico River the shallop was again at the mercy of the raging, ocean-like water. In the midst of a thunderous downpour the small craft was struck with such force and fury by the waves that her foremast was blown overboard and the men, soaked through, had to labor at bailing out the water to keep her from sinking. They were finally able to take refuge on one of an uninhabited group of islands, and here for two days the dripping trees afforded some shelter from the rain that continued to pour down upon them. It was an experience they wanted to forget, so they named these islands the Limbo Isles.

The explorers sailed on, with a new foresail made from their shirts, and came to an island inhabited by friendly savages who talked much of a mighty nation called the Massawomekes. Thereafter Captain John Smith was on the lookout for these mortal enemies of the weaker tribes of the Chesapeake.

Discouraged by the lack of fresh water and finding the Eastern Shore shallow and cut up by so many broken isles, they turned the shallop toward the Western Shore, crossing at a point where the bay was so wide the high cliffs on the other side could hardly be seen. There they anchored for the night and named the shelter Richards Cliffs.

And now Captain Smith began to have trouble on board the boat. The men wanted to return to the fort. They were weary of the hardships, sick of the discomforts, and wanted no more of the wet, rotten bread, not even if they starved! The Captain appealed to them as men, though he privately remarked that the "gallants" had expected he would hasten back after a few days' sailing.

Having spoken of the shame it would be to return with so little accomplished, he continued, "You cannot say but I have shared with you of the worst that is past; and for what is to come, of lodging, diet, or whatsoever, I am contented for you to allot the worst part to myself. As for your fears that I will lose myself in these unknown, large waters, or be swallowed up in some stormy gust, abandon those childish fears, for worse than is past cannot happen, and there is as much danger to return as to proceed forward. Regain therefore your old spirits, for return I will not (if God assist me) till I have seen the Massawomekes, found the Potomac, or the head of this great water which you think to be endless."

More disheartening days of foul weather followed, and some of the men fell sick, but they stopped grumbling, and on June 16th even the gallants regained the old spirit of adventure. For on that fair day they sailed up the broad, beautiful Potomac River. Little streams and sweet springs flowed down from the wooded hills to empty their waters into the stately river that was inhabited on both sides by many Indian tribes, including the Patawomeckes from whom the river took its name.

John Smith wanted to know the inhabitants as well as the land and the waters, and by now he knew how to cope with savages, friendly or unfriendly. So they explored the small rivers and streams and the inlets of the Potomac, seeking out the tribes that lived near-by.

All was peaceful one day while they were sailing up a deep creek when suddenly there arose the hideous shouting and yelling that told them they had been ambushed by Indians. The Captain and his men were quick to put the fear of the whiteman's firearms in them. The quiet waters splattered with bullets, echoes of the loud reports of the muskets rang back from the woods —and down came the bows and arrows of the painted devils.

After this kind of exclamatory introduction the palefaces would be conducted to the king's habitation where there would be a friendly exchange of courtesies and presents and conversation. In this region most of the conversation had to be carried on with the help of interpreters, for few of the tribes spoke the language of Powhatan which John Smith had mastered. The Indians themselves did not know all the different languages that the many tribes spoke.

Sometimes the Englishmen heard exciting news— will-o'-the-wisp reports of glittering metals and the mythical sea which always seemed to lie just beyond some barrier. Here a friendly tribe told of the shining ore the Patawomeckes mined. They found the mine, after tramping ten miles up into the country from the river, but the mineral was nothing but antimony and of no value to them.

Otters and beavers and martins and sables they saw in the woods, but it was the unbelievable abundance of fish they found in Chesapeake Bay and its adjacent waters that amazed them most. "There they were lying thick with their heads above water," the Captain said. "We had no nets, so we tried to catch them with a frying pan." The frying pan didn't work, so when they spied them lurking by the hundreds in shallow water near the entrance to the Rappahannock, Captain Smith set all the men to fishing with their swords. This worked so well that in an hour they had speared more fish than they could eat, but the Captain himself had a bad experience with one flailing fellow he was taking from his sword. It happened to be a stingeray, and the poisoned jab the fish gave John Smith's wrist—the Captain vowed the stinger went in an inch and a half!—caused such an alarming swelling of his hand, arm, shoulder and part of his body that he concluded death was near and gave instructions for his grave to be prepared on a near-by island. Death from a stingeray after all the hairbreadth escapes he had had from Turks and pirates and savages! But fate was not that unkind to the great adventurer. Dr. Russell applied a rare oil he carried in his medicine kit and by night the pain was so well assuaged that Captain John Smith made a hearty meal of the fish and named the island where he had expected to be buried Stingeray Isle.

And now they set sail southward for Jamestown. At Kecoughtan they stopped for a visit with the simple, friendly savages who stared at the Captain's swollen arm, at the bloody cut on the shin of one of the company, and at what looked to them like war booty: bows, arrows, targets, mantles, furs. With whom had the palefaces fought? "The Massawomekes," Captain John Smith promptly answered, knowing the advantage of keeping them in awe and fear of the white man. "And," he reported later, "the rumor went faster up the river than our shallop."

Arriving at the fort on July 21st, the Captain found nothing but misery and trouble. Many of the settlers were sick and the rest bruised, lame, and seething with complaints. President John Ratcliffe had lived riotously on the food stores and had brought the men to all their misery by forcing them to build him a "palace" in the woods. They were ready to torment him with revenge, but, heartened by the good news their Captain brought of his discoveries and of the hope that the great Bay stretched to the South Sea, they relented on the condition that Ratcliffe be deposed and Captain John Smith be named president.

The Captain was not yet ready to take over this official position of leadership, but he promptly took matters into his own hands. John Ratcliffe was ousted and Master Scrivener, Captain Smith's good friend, appointed to take his place. Honest officers were elected to assist him and order in general restored to the fort. Then the Captain got ready to set sail again to finish his exploration after telling the men that, considering their weakness and the heat of the season, they might live at ease during his absence.

Of the twelve men who sailed with Captain Smith on his second expedition on July 24th, some were from the old company and some newly recruited. Fairer weather favored this second voyage, and, sailing up the Western Shore, they arrived finally at the head of the Bay.

It was here that Captain Smith first encountered the notorious Massawomekes. Far across the waters he and his men saw seven or eight canoes filled with savages who seemed to be preparing to attack them. Quickly the number of men on the shallop multiplied. By the Captain's clever ruse of mounting all available hats on sticks and oars! And thus reinforced the explorers sailed on to meet the enemy.

But the enemy retreated to the shore, and here the shallop presently pulled up a short distance from them. Neither group showed any disposition to fight, and finally two of the redskins paddled over to the boat unarmed. They were received with signs of friendship and each given a shiny copper bell. Even the savage heart of a Massawomeke could be won by the presents the paleface Santa Claus pulled from his bag! Soon the rest of the Indians were swarming over the boat showering their own gifts upon the friendly palefaces—venison, bear meat and bear skins, bows and arrows and targets. By signs, and the evidence of fresh wounds, they let it be known that they had recently been at war with the Tockwoghs. Night fell and they shoved off in their canoes after promising to come again the next morning, but that was the last the explorers saw of them.

But now the Englishmen were armed with a subtle weapon—they carried the bows and arrows of the feared Massawomekes. When they entered the Tockwogh River they were surrounded by a fleet of canoes manned by Tockwogh warriors, some of whom came aboard the shallop for a friendly parley. One among them could speak the language of Powhatan, and Captain John Smith lost no time in telling him, who then told his fellow warriors, that the Massawomeke weapons, which their sharp black eyes had at once noted, had been won in a victorious encounter.

This fiction had the effect that Smith intended. The English explorers, so few in number, were conducted as conquerors to the palisaded town of the Tockwoghs. Here, in the Indian houses mantled with bark, mats were ceremoniously spread for them to sit upon and they were entertained with dancing and singing and feasted with bread, fish and the fruits of the land. Around them the observant Englishmen saw many hatchets, knives and odd pieces of brass and iron which intrigued their curiosity. The warrior who spoke Powhatan's language told Captain Smith they had got them from the Susquehannas, a mighty people who were also the mortal enemies of the Massawomekes.

The Susquehannas—the very name had a mighty sound, and Captain John Smith could not rest until he had met them. But the passageway that led up into their country was too rocky for the shallop. So the Captain persuaded his Tockwogh friend to go as a messenger with an interpreter to invite some of the Susquehanna warriors to come down for a friendly visit. The great river upon which they lived, and to which they had given their name—the Susquehanna—flowed down from the mountains to the north and emptied its waters into the Chesapeake at its head.

Four days later they came, sixty giant-like braves loaded with presents of venison, skins, tobacco pipes, baskets, targets, and bows and arrows. "Such great and well-proportioned men as we had seldom seen," the admiring Captain said of them, "and it seemed they were of an honest and simple disposition."

The Englishmen stared at them incredulously, for they were not only superior in stature, but were the strangest of all the natives they had met in this new land both in language and in dress. To John Smith's ear, so keenly sensitive to strange tongues, their speech matched their noble proportions. "As they spoke it," he said, "it sounded like a great voice in a vault or cave— as a mighty echo."

The Susquehannas revealed themselves as a people of imagination in their strange attire. They had seen possibilities in the skins of animals that less imaginative tribes had not perceived. A warrior wore a great bear's skin cut to slip over his head and fit to the waist as a kind of bodice. It was in the detail that his flair for design was shown. Loose fitting, cape-like sleeves hung to his elbows and were finished off at the gathered ends with the bear's paws. The animal's head was kept as part of the jacket and hung over the warrior's abdomen with another paw hanging like a pendant from the nose. The lower part of his body was covered with a fringed, draped skin, and around his neck hung a heavy chain to which was attached a wolf's head.

This mighty brave wore his hair long on one side and close shaven on the other up to the rolled ridge that curved over the crown of his head like a cock's comb. He carried his long flint or stone-headed arrows in a wolf's skin at his back. And the bow that he held in one hand and the club in the other were such as no warrior of Powhatan's tribes had ever handled. The pipe that he smoked was also unlike any other's. It was almost a yard long and the bowl was beautifully carved with some bird or beast. Heavy enough, the Captain observed, to beat out the brains of a man.

Five of the Susquehanna werowances were on board the shallop during their visit at the hour when the Englishmen had their daily prayer and psalm reading. And nothing about the palefaces so amazed these great chieftains as this simple service to the Christians' God. But even in the matter of worship they were not to be outdone. No sooner was the last prayer of the Christian explorers finished than the werowances turned to the sun and, stretching their powerful bronze arms upward in an attitude of adoration, began to sing with such intensity of feeling in their strange language that the Christians were awed, and declared it was a most fearful song.

The savages' declaration of love for their new-found, paleface friends was awesome, too. In like manner they now flung out their arms to Captain Smith and his men, and, twisting their bodies in frenzied contortions, began singing in praise and love of them. When this weird ceremony was finished, one among them came forward and draped a great painted bear's skin over the Captain's shoulders and hung a heavy chain of white beads around his neck. Would he not be their governor? Would he not come to their country and defend them against their hated enemies the Massawomekes? But the Captain felt the Susquehannas were quite able to take care of themselves and he had no wish to become one of them, so the palefaces took leave of them at Tockwogh after promising to visit them the next year.

And now, after having nosed into so many inlets, bays and rivers at the head of the Chesapeake, the shallop swung southward for the return voyage. Two important rivers were discovered and explored on the way back to Jamestown—the Patuxent, north of the Potomac, and the Rappahannock south of it. Up near the head of the Rappahannock, Richard Fetherstone, one of the gentlemen who had fallen ill, died. His body was lowered into the waters of a bay in the night as the men fired a volley of farewell to him. This bay they named Fetherstone Bay. Richard Fetherstone was the only man Captain John Smith lost on his two hazardous expeditions in the summer of 1608.

On September 7th the Jamestown settlers welcomed back the explorers of the Chesapeake. Master Scrivener and many others had recovered from summer illnesses, some were dead and some were sick, and the late President was a prisoner on a charge of mutiny. The rain had spoiled some of the stored food, but Master Scrivener, despite his illness, had been diligent in gathering the harvest, so there was no immediate want.

It had not been too bad a year, all things considered. The outstanding event and achievement had been Captain John Smith's two expeditions of exploration of Chesapeake Bay. No glittering mines of gold had been discovered and the South Sea was still as far away as it had always been, and always would be. But a great area of land and water had been opened up to Englishmen by John Smith's bold initiative. With good reason his men asked, "Who else with such small means did ever discover so many fair and navigable rivers?"

CHAPTER VIII *The English Crown
Powhatan*

"BY WHAT RIGHT can we enter into the land of these savages, take away their rightful inheritance from them, and plant ourselves in their places, being unwronged or unprovoked by them?"

That was a question which troubled a good many Englishmen. Those who were promoting American settlement felt they *did* have this right for a number of reasons. America was a land of almost unlimited extent and sparsely settled by a primitive people who had done nothing to develop its rich resources. What the English wanted was not to take the land away from the Indian but to share it with him, and in so doing bring to him the benefits of what they thought was a better way of life. One of the benefits would be the development of profitable trade, and this was a right which all nations had always recognized. But the most telling argument in support of the right of the English to enter the land of these savages was that if they didn't the Spanish or the French would. And there was no question in their minds as to who would be the better benefactor.

So the English came with the intention, and not too much troubled in conscience, of implanting the true faith among the heathen savages when the time was right for it. The time for serious missionary effort, they felt, would be after they had become well established in well fortified settlements. For the English promoters knew the nature of that native American. They knew he was a savage and would have to be dealt with as such. But in the meantime the settlers could help along the civilizing process by precept and good example. To that end they were admonished by the royal Council to be always just and kind in their dealings with the natives, or suffer severe penalties to be fixed by the resident council if they weren't. Then, after having been given specific instructions on how to protect themselves in all circumstances, they were told that if, after good and fair means had been used, the natives should barbarously respond with violence, it would be no breach for the settlers to defend themselves.

This restraint imposed by the royal Council irked no one so much as Captain John Smith. And because the Indians, most frequently inspired by Powhatan's treacheries and villainies, were an ever-present threat to the peace and safety of the colonists, he was often at odds with the Council as to how they should be treated.

[83]

He scoffed at the command from England not to offend them, and declared the Jamestown authorities would rather be anything than peace-breakers. The practical and realistic Captain knew that kindness and forgiveness was no way to deal with savage people who were inconstant in everything except when constrained by fear, and who were quickly moved to anger and so malicious that they seldom forgot an injury, real or imagined.

The Indians' petty thieving and pilfering was a frequent source of irritation to the harassed colonists, for they came often to the fort and it was their habit to take anything, but tools particularly, that they could seize. And their werowances were glad to receive the stolen goods. Only the Pamunkeys, Captain Smith found, did not steal. He also observed that, unless they were punished, and severely at that, he who stole today dared come on the morrow to steal again. So, without too much concern for what the Council at home or abroad thought, he set out to put the fear, not of God, but of Captain John Smith in their hearts. He hunted them up and down the island and when caught terrified them with sound beatings and imprisonment.

The old Emperor up on the York did not fool John Smith either with his gifts and assurances of love and friendship. Smith thought Captain Christopher Newport had been very unwise in sending him the twenty swords and when, after Newport's departure, Powhatan sent a big load of turkeys down to the fort for himself, the Captain did not respond with the weapons the wily old chief wanted and expected.

Powhatan promptly retaliated, determined to obtain the swords by trickery and treachery. Following several encounters with his redskins caught snooping around the fort, Smith and Master Scrivener were working in the cornfield one day when they saw two Indians approaching. Each was freshly painted and armed with a cudgel. "They came circling around me," the Captain said, "as though they were going to club me like a hare." To prevent more trouble, he called Master Scrivener and together they went back to the fort.

The savages followed and were joined by two others, also armed with clubs, who came up from the other side of the fort. After their admittance there was an argument about some Indians who were being held prisoners, and Smith, his patience finally exhausted, ended it by clapping them into prison, too. Powhatan craftily kept up this war of nerves from his throne-room up at Werowocomoco until even the president and the councilors were exasperated beyond endurance. They handed over the prisoners, who had sulkily refused to talk, to Captain John Smith with instructions to pry loose their secrets by whatever treatment he thought necessary.

Threat of the rack and then death by shooting or hanging from the Captain was enough so to frighten the savages that in a short time he had a full confession from them. He learned what he had suspected all along, that Powhatan was directing the Paspaheghs and the Chickahominies, his subjects, in a subtle plot not only to get possession of the swords of the settlers but to cut the throat of every colonist with them. After that the prisoners went submissively to morning and evening prayers; and somehow word reached the Emperor that all was not going according to plan. And then, as he had done before and would do again, he pretended innocence and begged for the release of his imprisoned warriors.

The lovely Pocahontas herself came as her father's emissary. She was not an unfamiliar figure at the fort, for she had come many times since the day when Captain John Smith was led a bound captive into the Emperor's presence. She had come as a friend of the white settlers, sometimes to relieve their hunger with generous gifts of food, at others to warn them of danger. And all because of Captain Smith. The wild-spirited nature of this Indian girl who turned cartwheels in the market place at Jamestown had responded quickly to the courageous and adventurous Captain, and he had found her, in feature and in countenance, in wit and in spirit, unlike any other among her people. And there had grown between them a warm and lasting friendship.

Pocahontas came on this mission accompanied by one of her father's most trusted messengers. Rawhunt was a deformed runt of an Indian, but he was crafty and shrewd like his master. With deference he laid the Emperor's gifts before Captain John Smith—a slain buck and baskets of freshly baked bread. Then he said, "The great Powhatan loves and respects you, Captain Smith. There is no reason for you to suspect his kindness—look, he has sent his dearest child to see you."

There were messengers from Opechancanough, too,

pleading for the release of his friends. As tokens of his good faith, he had sent the Captain his shooting glove and bracer, which was a covering for the arm to protect it from the vibrations of the bow's string.

Captain John Smith, who had once been the helpless prisoner and was now the judge, listened patiently to all the pleaders, accepted their gifts and then sent them back to their werowances to report that for the sake of Pocahontas the prisoners would shortly be given their liberty. On an afternoon following prayers, which the Indian prisoners attended, their bows and arrows were returned to them, and, in the custody of Pocahontas and Rawhunt, they were granted the freedom to return to their homes. Pocahontas accepted the gifts Captain Smith pressed upon her and promised to report to her father that the prisoners had been kindly treated.

Well might the Captain crow that, though not a man had been slain, yet the Indians had been brought to such a state of fear and obedience that his very name was enough to frighten them!

On September 10, 1608, this great leader who more than once had saved the Jamestown settlement from failure became president of the council. There was no slackening of his energy. Cool weather had come again and Captain Newport was on his way over with the second supply. New buildings to house the colonists he would bring were constructed, the storehouse was given a new roof and repairs were made on the church. All was in readiness when Newport's ship arrived early in October.

That was really a Day in the drab, overworked lives

of the Jamestown settlers, for this was no ordinary shipload of more men and more food and drink. On this October day when the Virginia woodlands were splashed with scarlet and gold the first woman to set foot on Jamestown Island daintily lifted her voluminous skirts and stepped off the boat with her maid. Mistress Forrest and Anne Burras had arrived. The little settlement was not yet ready for the shiploads of women who would come later to make homes for all the men.

Captain Newport brought no heartening news about the cargo of gold he had taken to England. It had turned out to be nothing but the gilded dirt Captain Smith had said it was. But among the seventy new settlers were eight Dutchmen and Poles who knew how to make glass, pitch, tar and soap ashes. The adventurers in London were not disheartened. If they could not make quick returns on their investment from gold mines they would put the colonists to work on other projects —even something as prosaic as making soap ashes, which were wood ashes from which the lye used in soap-making was extracted.

But it was not easy to give up the glittering dream of gold mines and a passage to the South Sea. The adventurers still clung to it. Captain Newport had been ordered to explore the river above the falls on this trip and for the purpose had brought along a boat in five sections to be carried over the falls and assembled on the other side for the voyage to the South Sea. He had also been instructed to look for gold mines along the way.

And there was a copper crown for Powhatan and an imposing array of presents. The palefaces were going to crown the red chieftain at an impressive ceremony. Just what this was expected to make him was not clear. It also puzzled the old Emperor who was shrewd enough, however, to see quite clearly that the English were trying to win him over to their own designs.

They had been trying for a long time without success. Their plans for converting the Indians to Christianity and to their way of life—particularly to their way of holding land and developing trade—could not be accomplished as long as this most powerful Indian chief remained obstinately and troublesomely uncooperative.

Powhatan was urgently needed as an ally at this time for the English promoters were getting ready for a big recruitment campaign. They wanted to speed up colonization of Virginia by sending over more settlers than ever before—hundreds of them in a fleet of ships. It would be much easier to persuade the English people to risk such a venture if they could be assured that the colonists and the natives were working and living harmoniously together.

So, more or less at their wits' end, the adventurers had hit upon this scheme of gaining prosperity and peace by appealing to the old Chief's childish vanity by staging a big coronation ceremony and showering him with presents.

Captain John Smith seemed to be the only one who knew Powhatan well enough to realize that he was not going to be hoodwinked by all this pageantry and hocus-pocus. He looked with a disdainful eye upon the presents—the basin, the ewer, the bed, the fine clothes and the plans to build the old warrior an English house. Smith knew they would never make an Englishman out of Powhatan. He was becoming skeptical, too, about finding the South Sea beyond the falls and laughed at Newport's sectional boat. He approved the hiring of the Dutchmen and the Poles, though; there was practical value in pitch, tar, glass and soap ashes.

But Smith was under orders to cooperate with Newport and his first assignment was to go to Werowocomoco to invite Powhatan to come down to Jamestown for his coronation and his presents. Accompanied by four men, he made the journey overland, and upon arrival learned that the Emperor was not at home. A messenger was dispatched, and while the Captain and his friends waited, the Indian women took advantage of the situation to put on a show of their own.

It was a surprise performance. Seated upon mats around a fire in a clearing among numerous men, women and children, the Englishmen were suddenly startled by such hideous shrieking and yelling coming from the surrounding forest that they supposed Powhatan had returned with his warriors and was there to attack them. But the savages gleefully shook their heads as Smith and his men reached for their arms. And presently thirty young Indian maidens came cavorting out of the woods so weirdly painted and adorned that they looked, as well as sounded, like fiends. All were horned with the stag's antlers and variously painted—some white, some red, some black, and others in a motley of colors. Their bodies were girdled with the skins of animals and each carried in her hand a sword, a club or a bow and arrows. They rushed forward with wild cries and shouts and flung themselves into a furious dance around the leaping flames. Finally, having exhausted themselves and the spectators as well, they dashed yelling back into the woods. Then everybody settled down to a feast of fruit, fish and wild game, beans, pease and bread.

The next day Powhatan returned, and Smith, in a formal and dignified manner, informed him of the great event and the presents awaiting him at Jamestown. He also added, as an afterthought, that Captain Newport was ready to set forth with him on the expedition of revenge that they had planned against the Monacans.

This time the old Chief was in no mood to beat about the bush with deceptive oratory. He was getting tired himself of this cat-and-mouse game with the English. He was in no mood either to capitulate.

Powhatan drew himself up to his full, regal height and made one of the few honest, forthright statements he had ever made to the paleface intruders. With simple dignity he said in reply to Captain John Smith: "If your King has sent me presents, I also am a king and this is my land. Eight days I will stay here to receive them. But your father is to come to me, not I to him, nor yet to your fort. Neither will I bite at such a bait. As for the Monacans, I can revenge my own injuries. And as to any salt water beyond the mountains, the reports you have had from my people are false."

This was the answer Smith took back to Captain Newport and there was nothing that crestfallen gentleman could do but load up and make the trip to Werowocomoco for the coronation. Three barges transported the crown, the clothing and the furniture, and Newport journeyed overland with a company of fifty armed men.

All went according to plan, and the day arrived when the stalwart braves and the painted maidens were assembled around the great throne-bed on which Powhatan sat in state and in style to receive the presents that were brought to him by Captain Newport and his men. The English furniture, looking quite outlandish among the savages and their trappings, was set up. Then the fine English apparel was laid out before Powhatan, but it was the rich scarlet cloak of velvet that brought the old Chief up from his bed. Assured that no harm lurked in its folds, he allowed the cloak to be draped over his shoulders.

While he was admiring himself in his regal robe, Captain Newport decided this was the right moment for the coronation. So the shining copper crown was brought forward and Newport, as master of the ceremony, indicated to the Emperor that he was to kneel to receive it. But at this the old Chief rebelled. The Englishmen concluded he did not know the meaning of either crown or the bending of the knee. It was probably the understanding, in his primitive way, that he was bending his knee to the English king that made the red chieftain a little wary. Was he not also a king? But having got this far the palefaces were not going to be balked, so when persuasion failed, they leaned hard on his shoulder and, having got him in a slightly stooped position, clapped the crown on his gray head.

There was a signal shot from the pistol of one of Newport's men and then such a deafening royal salute from the cannon on the barges down the river that the newly crowned Chief started forward in a terrible fright. After he had calmed down, having been assured that all was well, he thanked the Englishmen for their kindnesses and then, casting about for some token to express his appreciation, spied his mantle and a pair of old shoes which he gave to Captain Newport. But that was all. He would have no part in the attack on the Monacans; and after having attended to the dull business of trading for some corn, the coronation party returned to Jamestown.

But Newport had the sectional boat and he had his orders from the London Council, so he got ready to undertake the exploration above the falls without Powhatan's aid. One hundred and twenty men were chosen to go along and all the councilors went, including Captain Waldo and Captain Wynne, the two new members. But Captain John Smith, the new President, stayed at the fort. He had his hands full with other matters.

In the meantime a house for the manufacture of glass was built, under the Captain's supervision, on a forest clearing about a mile from the fort on the other side of the isthmus. By the time Newport returned Captain Smith had the Dutchmen and the Poles busily at work making the glass, the pitch, the tar and the soap ashes they had been sent over to make. Captain Newport's expedition was a dismal failure. The boat hadn't worked and the Monacans had been neither friendly nor hostile. They had just been indifferent to these intruders who were so eagerly looking for a salt sea up in their territory. On the return trip the explorers had hunted hopefully for valuable mines but none had been found. They finally came back to Jamestown half-sick and disgruntled, and ready to admit that the President had been right all along about the venture.

Captain John Smith cured their complaints and their illnesses. He put them to work helping the Dutchmen and the Poles and started teaching the gallants himself how to cut down trees and make clapboards. When they swore with every third blow because the axes blistered their tender hands he had a cure for that, too. He had every man's oaths numbered and in the evening, after the day's work was done, a can of water was poured down the sleeve of each man for every oath he had uttered.

So the day came when Captain Christopher Newport again sailed back to England, this time with a cargo of glass, pitch, tar, soap ashes and—clapboards.

CHAPTER IX *Troubles Plague the Settlers*

IN TAKING STOCK of the provisions that were left after Captain Newport's departure in November, the new President made an alarming discovery. Neither he nor the rest of the settlers had paid much, if any, attention to some passengers that were not listed on the supply ships: rats! Rats had been stowaways on those ships. They had disembarked with the others at Jamestown and scurried for the storehouse. There they had multiplied, and when Captain Smith came to see how much food was on hand for that winter of 1608-1609 he found to his horror that much of it had already been consumed by the rats. Worms were boring in, too, and the summer's rains had leaked through the roof and made a moldy mess of some of the provisions.

There were about two hundred people at Jamestown, including the new colonists that had come over on the last supply ship, who would have to be fed through the winter. It was a crisis in which the threat of famine demanded immediate action, and Captain Smith took it with characteristic vigor and alacrity. Corn expeditions were organized and the country scoured far and near for what grain could be obtained from the natives' supply. The Chickahominies were visited. Master Scrivener went in command of two barges and the pinnace to Powhatan's capital. Captain Wynne searched the country of the Nansemond Indians. The results of these and other foraging expeditions were desperately discouraging. In some places they found the savages more in the mood to fight than to trade. In others the inhabitants had fled, leaving empty dwellings and storehouses.

Captain Smith was grimly aware of the meaning of this failure to find food. It had been a bad year for corn and the improvident natives had stored very little. And Powhatan, in a thoroughly bad mood, was taking advantage of the general scarcity of grain to starve the colonists. Everywhere the foragers had learned that the refusal of the Indians to trade had been at the old Chief's command.

And now in the midst of the prevailing gloom wedding bells rang in Jamestown for the first time! John Laydon, a laborer and one of the few surviving first settlers, fell a victim to the charms of Anne Burras. So

Mistress Forrest lost her maid when the first Church of England wedding was solemnized there in the little Jamestown church. For better, for worse, John and Anne were going to face it together.

The wedding over and the crisis still with them, the President resolved to set out himself for a surprise visit to Powhatan to take by force, if necessary, some of his corn, when a messenger arrived from Werowocomoco. He brought the promise of a shipload of corn from the Emperor if Smith would send men to build a house for him and would bring him a grindstone, fifty swords, some guns, and a cock and a hen along with some beads and copper articles.

The Captain had little faith in Powhatan's promises, but conditions at the fort were so serious that he could not afford to neglect any opportunity for help. So, leaving Master Scrivener in charge, he and forty-six men boarded the pinnace and two barges on December 29th and turned downstream for Werowocomoco. Four of the Dutchmen and two Englishmen had been sent overland to build the house for the Emperor.

A winter of bitter cold had already set in, and sleety gales compelled them to seek shelter ashore at Kecoughtan. They spent a week or longer in the warm, smoky houses of these friendly savages making merry with them during the Yule season, and feasting on fish, oysters and wild fowl. "Do not trust Powhatan," the Kecoughtans warned Smith and his men. "He has sent for you only to cut your throats."

But the Captain preferred the risk of having his throat cut to starving, so he continued on his way when the weather cleared, and arrived at Werowocomoco on January 12th. There they found the river so clogged with ice and frozen slush off-shore that the men had to walk almost waist-deep for a half mile. They were grateful for Powhatan's hospitality—the warm quarters and the plenty of bread and venison he sent them.

The next day Captain Smith had an audience with the Emperor. He found him the same wily old fox. He had not sent for the Englishmen. He had little enough corn, but for forty swords he would part with forty bushels. Smith reproached him for being so forgetful, but his only answer was croaky laughter. Then he scowled and declared he would bargain for nothing but swords and guns.

Thoroughly exasperated the Captain replied, "Believing your promise to supply my wants, I have neglected everything to come here. I have sent you men to build your house. As for the swords and guns, I told you long ago that I have none to spare. What I have can keep me from want, though. You have forbidden your people to trade with us and now you think that by consuming our time we shall be consumed by want."

The wrangling went on and on from one day to the next. Powhatan accused the Captain of coming, not to trade, but to attack his people and take possession of his land. "To relieve us of this fear," he said, "leave your weapons aboard, for here they are needless, we being all friends and forever Powhatans." With dogged cunning the old Emperor harped upon this note in all his conversations and dealings with his paleface adversary.

"Come unarmed to us and supply us with your weapons." Smith was no fool—and he knew as well as Powhatan how to fence with words.

At last they began to trade and the Captain succeeded in getting a fair store of corn in return for the beads and the copper, the grindstone, and the cock and the hen he had brought. Too much time had already been consumed, and while Powhatan continued to complain in a querulous voice, Captain Smith ordered some of the savages down to the river to break the ice so one of the barges could come for him and the corn. He also sent an order for the rest of his men to come ashore.

And then it happened as it always did. The savages struck with the suddenness and unexpectedness of storm-lightning. Powhatan had mysteriously disappeared and the room was filled with naked devils bent upon braining Smith and his handful of men with their clubs and hatchets. But the Captain could strike back as swiftly, and he and his soldiers were armed with pistols and cutting swords. A few shots and a few passes were enough to scatter the savages. Nobody was hurt, and presently the grim natives were tamely bearing the Captain's corn down to the barge on their backs.

One of the Emperor's ancient orators was on hand to explain the incident. "Captain Smith," he croaked, "our werowance fled because he feared your guns. Knowing that when the ice was broken more of your men would come, he sent his warriors to guard his corn from the pilfering that might happen without your knowledge. Yet he is your friend and will so continue. If you would have his company, send away your arms which so frighten his people they dare not come to you." And then he presented the Captain with a bracelet and a chain of pearls in token of the Emperor's enduring love and friendship.

A pretty little conspiracy was already afoot by the time Captain John Smith nosed down the slushy river away from Werowocomoco. The Dutchmen, hirelings with no love for the English, had taken stock of the situation and decided their future looked brighter with old Powhatan. Famine and danger faced them at Jamestown; plenty and the protection of Powhatan's warriors at Werowocomoco. Smith's boats were hardly out of sight when two warriors set forth for Jamestown to procure the arms he had refused the Emperor. There they told a plausible story to Captain Wynne and Master Scrivener, made confederates of a half dozen of Captain Smith's enemies and returned to Werowocomoco with the swords, guns, hatchets, powder and shot that Powhatan so coveted.

Meanwhile Captain Smith had arrived in the country of the Pamunkeys up on the Pamunkey River. Opechancanough, the werowance and Smith's one-time captor, had been well coached by his brother, the old Emperor. There was the same show of hospitality, the same time-consuming bickering, and, Smith began to suspect, the same plot to trap and slay himself and his men.

Suddenly the Captain, in the midst of a heated argument, threw caution to the winds and in a rage seized Opechancanough by a tuft of hair, and pressing his pistol against the King's naked breast shouted, "You

Pamunkeys promised to freight my ship ere I departed, and so you shall, or I mean to load her with your dead bodies."

This reckless act of bravery so frightened Opechancanough and his warriors that they tremblingly dropped their weapons and began heaping corn into baskets which they carried down to the waiting barges.

Smith ranged the Pamunkey country for a week. It was evident that Opechancanough's people did not want to fight, and, having heard the story of the Captain's defiance of their Chief, they came willingly across the frost-bitten fields bearing as much corn on their naked backs as they could reasonably spare from their scant supplies.

It was at this time that a messenger came from the fort bringing sad news to Captain John Smith. His good friend Matthew Scrivener, along with Captain Waldo and nine others, had been caught in a violent squall about seven miles from Jamestown, their overloaded boat had capsized, and every man aboard had drowned. The Captain concealed his grief and cautioned the messenger to keep news of the loss secret. The settlement had lost one of its best men and John Smith had suffered a deeper personal loss in the death of his man Friday, but the work of keeping the rest alive had to go on.

The corn hunters next searched the countries of Youghtamund and Mattapony where they found the savages friendly and ready to share what they had, but so poor in grain that freezing winter! On the chance that he might be able to induce Powhatan to let him have a little more corn, Smith decided to stop by Werowocomoco again on the way back. Upon arrival he sent two of his men to apprise the Emperor of his return visit, but they were soon back with the report that he had abandoned his new house and Werowocomoco and had moved his seat of government to Orapakes, a town farther west on the Chickahominy River. The old Emperor had long felt he was too close to Jamestown for comfort and the Dutchmen had convinced him he was right and had persuaded him to make the move at this time. They, too, wanted to be a safer distance from the Captain's headquarters. So, early in February, Captain Smith returned to Jamestown and delivered the two hundred seventy-nine bushels he had collected at such hazard and risk and with so much effort.

But there was no rest even now for him: "We returned to find nothing done," he complained, "the victuals spent and most of our tools and a good part of our arms conveyed to the savages." The culprits who were sneaking out the weapons and the tools to Powhatan's Dutchmen could not be detected at once, but the shiftless and the lazy could be put to work.

The Captain stored the corn, forgetting about the rats, it seemed, and went to work on the shirkers. They had to listen to a long speech by their President that ended with this stern warning: "Seeing now that the authority rests wholly in myself, you must obey this for a law: that he who will not work shall not eat." Most of them began to hustle, and those who didn't were severely punished.

The house over on the mainland where the Dutchmen and the Poles were making glass had come to be called the glass-house, and now the alert Captain began to get wind of strange goings-on up there—of activities having nothing to do with the manufacture of glass. In time he learned that it had become the rendezvous of the four Dutchmen at Werowocomoco and their conniving confederates at Jamestown. He learned, too, that on a certain day one of the stout Dutchmen was coming down, disguised as a savage, to find out why instructions from headquarters were not being followed. Smith did not know, however, that forty of Powhatan's men, including the King of the Paspaheghs, were coming with the Dutchman to lie in ambush.

On the appointed day Captain Smith marched up to the glass-house with twenty armed men, intending to arrest the villain. He was not there. Thinking he was on his way back to Powhatan, Smith sent his soldiers after him and started back to the fort alone armed only with a falchion, a broad, short sword that curved sharply to the point.

And suddenly, there in the woods near the river, he encountered Wochinchopunck, King of the Paspaheghs. That swarthy savage attempted to lure him into the ambush, and failing in that, took a shot at the Captain with a stolen pistol he carried. The shot missed and Smith, having no time to draw his falchion, leaped upon the King and grappled with him.

In the terrific struggle that followed, the stalwart savage succeeded in forcing Smith into the river where he intended to drown him. But, while they continued to lunge and grapple in the water, Wochinchopunck saw two Poles approaching and tried to flee. Smith grabbed him by the hair and throat and held him until the Poles arrived. Begging for his life now, he was escorted at the curved point of the Captain's falchion to the fort where he was fettered and locked up.

Then, soon afterwards, the soldiers came in with the Dutchman they had caught tearing back to Powhatan. Shaking with fear, he began explaining, in a mixture of Dutch and English, how he had been forced to give Powhatan the weapons, how he had escaped at the risk of his life and that he was out in the woods gathering walnuts when the soldiers laid hold of him. The chains were snapped on and, for all his explaining and pleading, he was clapped into prison, too.

And now Captain Smith's plan was to offer to spare Wochinchopunck's life if the rest of the Dutchmen were returned. The King himself sent messengers from the fort to Powhatan, imploring him to send them back that he might return safely to his people. But word came that they wouldn't budge and that they were too great a burden for the warriors to carry so many miles overland on their backs from Orapakes.

The King's wives, children and his people, the Paspaheghs, began coming daily with presents—patient files of them trailing silently down through the woods to the fort. And still the prisoner sat chained in his dark cell, but always watchful, his black eyes darting in all directions. And one day the guard was careless and he saw his chance to escape. With bound hands, he glided through the partly opened door and disappeared like a shadow into the deep woods.

Captain John Smith was absent from the fort at the

time this happened. When he returned and learned of the King's escape and of Captain Wynne's unsuccessful efforts to recapture him, he was angry. He was so angry that he went on the warpath himself with a company of tough soldiers. Again he went up and down the island and beyond tracking down those who, at Powhatan's instigation, were making life both miserable and dangerous for the colonists. Some he killed and some he took prisoners. He burned their houses, carried off their boats and all their fishing equipment and let it be known he would not cease to make war upon them until they were thoroughly chastised. And again the savages cowered with the fear of Captain John Smith in their hearts and begged for peace.

So the Captain came back to Jamestown with his men, thinking that Indian problems had been settled for a while and that now he could give his attention to much that had been neglected at the fort. But no. He had hardly taken off his helmet and laid aside his musket before he had to listen to the complaint that a young Chickahominy had stolen a pistol and some tools. John Smith's wrath flared up again and he set out in search of the culprit.

The thief could not be found, but two young Indians who were brothers and known to have been implicated in the theft were caught. One was sent for the pistol and warned to be back with it within twelve hours or his brother, who was kept prisoner, would be hanged.

It was a very cold night, and Smith, having some pity for the naked savage in the unheated cell, sent him food and charcoal for a fire.

Just before midnight the brother returned with the pistol, and the Captain, true to his word, conducted him to the cell to release the imprisoned Indian. They found the prisoner, to all appearances—dead! In the smoke-filled room he lay badly burned beside the fire, over which he seemed to have rolled, and unconscious. Smith himself at once concluded he had smothered to death. But in the interval during which the bereaved brother's cries and lamentations broke forth, he did some fast thinking. Maybe he wasn't dead—anyway he took a chance.

"If I bring your brother back to life," Captain Smith said to the wailing one, "will you promise that hereafter neither of you will ever steal again?" And, assured with much nodding of the head that they would forever afterward be good Indians, he went to work on the dead one.

Aqua vitae and vinegar were brought and the Captain poured this potent mixture down the throat of the unconscious savage. It worked. But he came back to life raving in such a demented manner that his frightened brother was again plunged into a torment of grief.

Captain Smith felt sure of himself now. So he again extracted the promise of never to steal again from the grieving brother if he cured the ailing one of his malady, and had him led away. Presently the lunatic quieted down and Smith stretched him out at a safe distance from the fire for sleep.

The next morning the young savage, having slept well, arose completely restored to both life and sanity.

And his awe-struck brother looked upon his recovery as a miracle. The Captain had the victim's burns dressed, gave each of the brothers a piece of copper and sent them on their way.

The news spread fast among the savage tribes. Captain John Smith could bring a dead man back to life! Even the old Emperor was awed and frightened. After that the few Indians who dared to steal from the colonists were sent back by their werowances with the stolen goods to Jamestown for punishment. And the miracle-working Captain could report later that "All the country became absolutely as free for us as for themselves."

Now the long-neglected work at the fort really got under way. The runaway Dutchmen did not return, but they no longer troubled the busy colonists. Those who had faithfully remained at the fort went to work up at the glass-house and, with the help of the Poles, began producing glass. Barrels were being filled with pitch and tar and soap ashes, too, and down in the fort the first well was dug.

The Captain strode over the island like the busy overseer he was, supervising first one thing and then another. The church, always in need of repairs in that humid climate, was given a new roof, and twenty new houses were built. Out in the woods, trees were crashing down to be sawn into clapboards and wainscot, and forty acres of ground were dug and planted.

Even the pigs and the chickens were doing their share. Five hundred chickens "brought up themselves" without a scrap from table or storehouse, and three sows produced sixty little pigs in one year! The hogs became so numerous that they were transported to an island of their own near-by, appropriately named Hog Island.

And then, when it seemed that at last the little settlement was going to flourish, the clouds began to gather again; one very dark cloud, rather, that began to shove up over the horizon and grow bigger and bigger. A time was at hand that became another epic chapter in human suffering.

The colonists didn't know it yet, but Captain John Smith must have had some fore-knowledge of it the day he went to the storehouse to look at the corn. With so much on his mind and so much to do he must have forgotten the rats. He thought of them too late. For that day he found that most of the corn that had been so laboriously gathered had been devoured by them. They were scampering about by the thousands—and there was no Pied Piper on Jamestown Island!

The black cloud pushed up a little higher and a little bigger above the horizon. Every settler, to the last man, even including the Captain, was at his wits' end. There was almost nothing to eat now except what nature provided. All work stopped and every man became a forager like a wild animal. Large numbers went down the river to the oyster beds and suffered a strange malady from eating too many and nothing but oysters. Their skin peeled off from head to foot!

The men searched for berries, acorns and roots, and fished for sturgeon. The sturgeon dried, pounded and mixed with herbs made a fairly edible bread, but it was a "trashy" diet, and the half-starved colonists rebelled. Again the sternest disciplinary measures were necessary. The Captain shared their lot, as he always had, and gave warning that, "Everyone who fails to gather each day as much as I do, the next day shall be set beyond the river and forever banished from the fort to live there or starve."

On July 13, 1609, the dreary and miserable monotony of their lives was broken, briefly, by the appearance of a strange ship that came slowly up the James and anchored alongside the fort. It was not a supply ship, but one, commanded by Captain Samuel Argall, that brought news from abroad and a little food. Captain Argall had been sent by the officers of the Company to find a more direct route to Virginia than the one usually taken by way of the West Indies. The belief had long been held that the Gulf Stream above Florida ran too strong for ships to cut across it safely. Captain Argall, keeping a course just south of the easterly flowing Gulf Stream, disproved this, and set a record by completing the voyage from England in sixty-nine days.

Of more interest to the settlers was the news that with the reorganization of the Company, there would be important changes in the government of the colony. Sir Thomas Gates had been commissioned the first governor and was probably already on the way over aboard one of a fleet of nine ships bringing several hundred new colonists.

But it is likely that the famished old settlers gave

little thought at the moment to this staggering news as they thirstily drank the wine and hungrily devoured the biscuits that Captain Argall generously handed out from an abundant supply.

CHAPTER X   *The Great Fleet Sails*

WHILE THE COLONISTS STRUGGLED during the spring of
1609 to give permanence to the Jamestown adventure,
the merchant-adventurers in London wrestled around
the conference table with the problems that were bog-
ging down the effort.

Something had to be done about the vexatious Indian
problem and the adventurers adopted some of the sug-
gestions offered by the settlers themselves. Powhatan's
influence had to be destroyed, and to accomplish this
they now planned to bring the tribes under English
control by requiring from each tribal chieftain annual
payments of corn, skins and dye materials. The colonists
were also to be instructed to make use of native labor
and to cultivate the friendship of tribes outside Powhatan's confederacy. To weaken the superstitious influence of the medicine men, they were to be encour-

aged to take young Indians, with parental consent, into their households to teach them the English language and the Christian way of life.

But drastic changes within the Company itself, and particularly in the management of the colony, were now recognized as urgently necessary. Accordingly, Sir Thomas Smith, one of London's greatest merchant-princes, appealed to the King through his ministers for a new charter. And on May 23, 1609, the royal seal was affixed to a second charter which was issued in the name of The Treasurer and Company of Adventurers and Planters of the City of London. Of adventurers *and* planters—the Virginia colonists would now share equally in the dividends. More important, they received recognition in this new charter which gave them the dignity of equality of status with the promoters in London who, however, still controlled their destiny.

The reorganized Company was now commonly called the Virginia Company, and its territorial boundaries in the new charter were extended to reach two hundred miles along the coast northward from Point Comfort, the same distance to the south and inland "from sea to sea, west and northwest." The Virginia Company would hold title to all the land, pay all expenses and receive all the profits from the labors of the planters for a period of seven years. At the end of that time the land which had been opened up and cultivated would be divided and every planter given at least one hundred acres with his own house, garden and orchard in return for his seven years of service to the Company. The colonists would continue to be dependent during this period on a common store into which would go the fruits of their various labors.

The Superior Council in England, now under control of the stockholders, remained essentially the same, but the affairs of the colony were to be administered in Jamestown by a single governor with almost unlimited power in place of the old local council in which no one had adequate responsibility or authority.

The Council was fired with ambitious plans and hopes for the little settlement which at this time was floundering in such a precarious condition. Great sums of money were needed to carry out these plans, and it had to come from subscribers to the joint-stock fund, people who would buy stock in the Company and thereby become adventurers. A vigorous campaign for subscriptions had been launched early in February before the new charter was issued, and there was enthusiastic response from all kinds and classes of people—the great lords, the bishops, the gentry, the merchants, widows, ministers, grocers and from the big City Companies of Brewers, Carpenters, Musicians, Fishmongers and many others.

The members of the Council came to the conclusion that what the colony needed most to become established on a firm footing was a great increase all at once in the number of planters. Too few new settlers had trickled in from the supply ships. So, under the able leadership of Sir Thomas Smith, who was the Treasurer and presiding officer of both the Council and the Company, preparations were made for sending out a great fleet to reach Virginia in the early summer.

While business representatives of the Company bargained with shipowners and shipmasters, the campaign to persuade people to risk such a venture was pushed forward. The printing presses hummed turning out broadsides and pamphlets in which all the attractive and alluring features of settlement in Virginia were set forth. Ministers spoke in behalf of it from their pulpits as a service to God and country. People responded—physicians, ministers, artisans, craftsmen, laborers, servants, gentlemen and soldiers.

In time five hundred men and about one hundred women and children volunteered to uproot themselves from their homeland and start life anew in the far, strange country of Virginia. They had made this weighty decision for various reasons. Some looked to the new country as already a land of opportunity where they hoped to improve their lot. Many hearkened to the old call of adventure and the promise of striking it rich without much effort. The skilled workers looked for more profitable employment than they were able to find at home. Then there were the foot-loose who were just looking for some other place to go, and the scapegrace sons whose fathers shipped them off.

And what would these six hundred new colonists do in Virginia besides make clapboards for the Company and trade trinkets with the Indians for corn to live on? The Council had given much thought to that. First of all, the planters were instructed, for reasons of security and the expansion of the colony, to establish two or three other settlements, or seats, besides that at Jamestown. As for the labor they would perform for the mutual advantage of the Company and themselves, the Council planned to direct and aid them along three broad lines. There was still a faint flicker of hope that the passage to the South Sea and the gold and silver mines would be found, and search for these was not to be abandoned. But the emphasis now was to be on manufacturing, trading with the natives and developing agriculture for commercial profit as well as for adequate subsistence. The adventurers were eager for the colonists to begin experimenting with various products. They had hopes and plans at this time for the production of silk, of sugar and of a good Virginia wine.

And while the members of the Council sat around the conference table talking plans and putting plans down on paper, all England was agog over the preparations for the sailing of the great fleet. There had never been anything like it before. Nine ships would carry eight hundred passengers and seamen three thousand miles across the Atlantic to a land called Virginia where a little English settlement called Jamestown had been planted in the wilderness among the savage inhabitants of that wild country.

A vast amount of equipment, as well as great numbers of planters to use it, were needed to tame both the natives and the land before civilization could begin to flourish there. So little thought was given to the comfort and accommodation of the men and women who were breaking up their homes and getting ready to sail on the long, perilous voyage. The carpenters who ham-

mered and sawed away down below decks were recon-
structing the ships for the cargoes of food and other
supplies that would have to be transported.

The day finally came when all was ready for the ship-
loaders—the husky, strong-muscled men who bore the
great loads of freight down into the holds of the vessels.
There was the storage space which came to look like an
arsenal after it had been filled with the ordnance: the
guns, the swords, the powder, the shot, and also other
kinds of ammunition the settlers needed to defend and
protect themselves and their homes.

So many and so many different kinds of tools had to
be taken to build houses and till the soil! Crated and
boxed and stowed away in other spaces were millstones
for grinding the grain, and grindstones for sharpening
the axes, adzes, hatchets, hammers, chisels, knives, files,
saws, pliers, reaphooks, scythes, trowels, wedges, shov-
els, spades, shears, augers, gimlets, vises and hoes.

Very little furniture was taken, for, with these tools
and the necessary skills in their strong hands, the men
could convert the great trees standing on the far shores
into what would be needed. But they had to take the
hardware for the homes they would build: andirons,
tongs, spits, nails, bolts, latches, hinges, door locks,
scales, pots, and pot hooks and racks.

They had to take stores of household goods and sta-
ples, too. Such needed supplies as thimbles, buttons,
needles and thread, dishes, bowls, spoons, kettles, la-
dles, frying pans, bottles, candles and candlesticks, bel-
lows, soap, chalk, rugs, mats, bolsters and bedding, and

paper, parchment and ink for written records of all kinds and the letters home.

And these emigrants from England had to be clothed as befitted civilized people in those days. So there were boxes and boxes in which were stored shoes, stockings, breeches, belts, shirts, hats, dresses, petticoats and many other articles of wear.

How important, too, were the precious supplies of seeds that they carried for planting immediately upon arrival. Seeds for parsnips, carrots, cabbages, turnips, lettuce and onions, that, with other varieties of the vegetables of their homeland, would supplement what they would find in the new country.

There was nothing so precious, though, as the food supplies, the food on which life itself would depend until the voyage was over and their first harvest gathered. In the ships' larders were cheese, fish, beef, pork, bacon, oatmeal, biscuit, bread, butter, peas, onions, raisins, prunes and dates. To make the food more appetizing, there were provisions of salt, pepper, sugar, cinnamon, clove, nutmeg, mace, vinegar and oil. And for liquid refreshment, cider, beer, the light-colored wine called sack, and aqua vitae, or alcohol.

Transporting livestock across the ocean was both difficult and expensive. Only a few animals were shipped on any one voyage, and these were used for breeding so that the stock would multiply in the colony. The Jamestown settlers had made a good start with hogs, chickens, sheep and cattle, but the planters about to set sail did not know that starvation had already depleted them. Little space was available on the nine vessels for animals, but somewhere room was found for six mares and two horses.

All was in readiness at last for the sailing of the fleet. Sir George Somers, grizzled old veteran of many sailings on many seas, was the admiral, and the vice-admiral was Captain Christopher Newport, who already knew the Atlantic and little Jamestown so well. Their flagship was a tall-masted vessel that bore the proud, bold name of *Sea Venture*. Lord Delaware, who had been elected Governor of the colony of Virginia, was unable to sail with Admiral Somers, but it was planned that he would follow in August in command of another fleet that would carry one thousand more planters. The great migrations to America that would continue unbroken for the next thirty years had begun.

Sir Thomas Gates, also a member of the Council, had been appointed to serve as the first Governor at Jamestown until the arrival of Lord Delaware. William Strachey had been elected to the position of secretary of the colony. Both these important officials sailed with Admiral Somers on the *Sea Venture*.

Little is known about the five hundred men and the one hundred women and children who sailed on those nine ships, for no personal records have been preserved. Doubtless each brought some hand luggage and a few boxes and parcels on shipboard. And tucked in somewhere with the few personal effects were probably cherished little keepsakes and mementoes of the life and the homes they had left. It is likely, too, that each carried his own pallet, or bedroll of some kind, for there were no sleeping quarters on the crowded ships, and at night they had to stretch out wherever space could be found to lie.

From various ports the nine vessels of Somers's fleet gathered in the harbor of Plymouth, and from there they set sail for the distant shores of Virginia on the morning of June 2, 1609. No risk could be taken on this momentous voyage of an encounter with hostile Spanish ships. So, instead of following the usual route by way of the West Indies through Spanish waters, the Admiral took a course similar to that which had been taken by Captain Samuel Argall.

Day after day and week after week the nine ships rode the swells of the Atlantic together, their white sails bellied by fair winds. The passengers grew weary of the unending reaches of the sea. They tired of the great sky that blazed with sunlight by day and glittered with millions of stars at night. They knew the misery of overcrowded daily living on ships that had not been equipped for even the most meager comforts of voyagers.

Seven weeks passed. And now, with the voyage almost over, their faces began to brighten. Soon they could begin to look hopefully each day out across the wide waters for the sight of land that had been lost to them for so long. Soon they could begin to expect, on any morning when they might still lie sleeping, the heart-lifting cry of "Land-Ho!"

And then it struck. On July 24th a mighty hurricane blew up out of the northeast and caught the nine ships squarely in its path.

CHAPTER XI *John Smith Departs*

DURING THE MONTH following Captain Samuel Argall's arrival in Jamestown on July 13, 1609, the colonists had much to think about besides the withering heat and their near-empty stomachs. There was more on Captain John Smith's mind. While the settlers daily looked down the river for sight of the ships bringing their first governor and the new planters, the Captain wrinkled his brow in worried thought over many problems. How would these several hundred new arrivals be fed when there were not enough provisions in the storehouse for the needs of the two hundred people already here? Where could shelter be found for them until many new houses could be built?

[120]

And, most disturbing of his thoughts, what would be his fate when some of his old enemies returned with a new government in the making? For Smith had learned from Captain Argall that three of his former fellow-councilors, with whom he had quarreled violently, were on their way back with Governor Gates. He looked forward with no pleasure to seeing again Captains Gabriel Archer, John Martin and John Ratcliffe, who had wanted to see him hanged. Furthermore, the forthright Captain already had about as many enemies in the colony as he could handle.

Days passed and the men grumbled and fretted and loafed listlessly in the shade of the big cypresses along the river bank and wagered how maybe all the ships had been sunk, they were so long coming. And then on the hot afternoon of August 11th, when the bees droned and a heavy somnolence hung over the fort, a shout suddenly went up from some watcher more alert than the rest. In a matter of seconds, every able man within earshot was at the river bank craning his neck to look downstream and trying to keep from being pushed into the water by those who crowded him from behind. "The ships! The ships are coming!" everyone was crying excitedly. And unmistakably they were, at least four of them, sailing slowly up the broad river.

And at last they arrived, four of Somers's storm-battered vessels. There was dazed disbelief on the faces of the half-famished men who gathered at the landings to welcome the first children and the first group of women to step ashore on their wilderness-island. There was utter bewilderment on the faces of the exhausted men, women and children who staggered up the tree-shaded paths to the little huddle of buildings around and inside the palisaded fort. This was Jamestown! This was the haven they had finally reached after the long, exhausting voyage and three days and four nights of storm-lashing terror, the memory of which caused even the bravest men to shudder.

But now it was good, solid earth on which they stood once more. And, though the heat was oppressive and Jamestown a dismal settlement—so unlike what they had expected—they were grateful. They were grateful, too, for the hospitality of the colonists who had so pitifully little to offer them.

How eager those half-starved, half-sick men were to hear about the perilous voyage that these newcomers had survived! And that evening they gathered in the cool, moonlit square to listen to the long story.

For the first time the Virginians learned that a fleet of nine vessels had sailed from Plymouth, England, on June 2nd. Nine ships! The settlers who had never seen half that many boats on the James at one time repeated the words unbelievingly. Then, even more astounding news! "Our flagship was the *Sea Venture*," a narrator said, "and aboard her were Admiral Somers, Vice-Admiral Newport, Governor Gates, Secretary Strachey and other important men."

"Coming *here?*" several of the old planters asked uncomprehendingly, all in a breath, as they looked around at the dilapidated buildings hemmed in by the black woods that seemed to crowd so threateningly close. But there was a note of hope in their voices, too. The big Company in London had not forgotten them!

"But what happened? What happened to the other ships?" they asked eagerly.

"We don't know," another newcomer, who broke in at this point, said. "All we know is that somehow, after the terrible hurricane finally died down and the sea became calm again, our four ships found one another and sailed on here together."

There was a kind of shuddering chorus among the voyagers of, "Oh—what a storm!" at mention of the hurricane. And then one who remembered most vividly what had happened, began to talk excitedly. "It roared up out of the great bright sky and out of the steel-blue sea," he said huskily. "In no time at all, mighty winds lifted the lazy swells of the ocean into pounding waves of staggering size. And black clouds rolled across the sky and blotted out all the light."

"And the thunder!" one of the women exclaimed in a high-pitched voice. "It cracked open the heavens and the way the rain poured down on us was like great rivers flooding our helpless ships from above."

"We didn't say anything," a little home-body of a woman said timidly. "We were afraid to talk—we just huddled close together and held on to each other when the ship lurched crazily. But I know we all prayed."

One of the strong, brawny seamen mumbled, "That old ocean rose up so high we couldn't see the top of her. Must have reached the clouds. And pretty soon we couldn't even see the other ships. It was black, I tell you, and after the fleet was driven apart it was every ship for itself."

"Yes, it was black," a new planter agreed thoughtfully. "It was so black that I think most of us gave up all hope of surviving the wild fury of wind and wave and thunderous downpour. But here we are, so mercifully preserved by God, and who knows? Perhaps the other ships of our fleet will also find their way to this safe harbor."

And about ten days later two more ships of the hurricane fleet *did* limp up the James. They roped alongside the four vessels that had preceded them and discharged another dazed group upon the already over-taxed little settlement. The problems of housing and feeding were becoming more and more acute, and official instructions for meeting the critical situation were lacking because the instructions and the principal officers were aboard, or had been aboard, the *Sea Venture*, and nobody—*nobody*—knew where the *Sea Venture* was.

Captains Archer, Martin and Ratcliffe had arrived and, as Captain John Smith had expected, they lost no time in stirring up a very hornets'-nest of trouble. "Never was there more confusion or misery," the harassed Captain exclaimed. His old enemies railed against him, made charges against, plotted against him. "They did their best," Smith said, "to make us all their servants and slaves."

Then there were, among the newly arrived settlers, "the unruly gallants who had been packed thither by their families and friends." They wanted to rule, too— to rule all or ruin all, as the Captain summed it up. Here was a pretty kettle of fish! With the fate of the colony hanging by a thread, just about everybody wanted to be the leader and hardly anybody wanted to acknowledge a superior! And, in the absence of the Governor and with no directions or instructions from the Council in London, there was no authority to which or to whom the harried colonists could appeal. At least, under the provisions of the old charter, Captain John Smith had the legal right to his office as President of the local council and the Captain held on to it in spite of the determined efforts of his enemies to dislodge him.

News of this state of affairs in the colony was going out daily by the grapevine route to the Indian towns where trouble for the settlers was beginning to brew again. The unruly gallants knew nothing of Indian diplomacy and became quite reckless in their relations with the savages. Smith's sympathies this time were all on the side of the natives. "The disorderly company so tormented those poor naked souls," he said, "by stealing their corn, robbing their gardens, beating them and keeping some prisoners that they daily complained that I had brought them for protectors worse enemies than the Monacans."

And then, in the midst of all the turmoil and confusion, Mr. Francis West, a younger brother of Lord Delaware, decided it was the right time to take a company of one hundred and twenty men up to the falls to start a new settlement there. And Captain Martin set off with about the same number to pay a dubious visit to the Nansemond Indians in their town on the Nansemond River.

Soon after West and Martin had left on these ill-advised ventures, Captain John Smith sailed up the James on his last mission for the shaky little settlement. He was on his way to the falls to see how West and his men were faring up there. He found them building a fort at a location where Richmond now stands.

It was not, in Smith's judgment, a suitable place for a seat, and he tried to persuade West to follow other plans. They argued violently, and finally the Captain, in disgust, was on his way back to Jamestown. He had not sailed far when his boat grounded and word reached him that the emboldened savages had attacked both West's company at the falls and Martin's group in the Nansemond country. Many of the men in both companies had been slain and the infuriated natives were still on the warpath. The Captain tarried at this spot long enough to make a temporary peace with the Indians and to try once more to persuade West to give up the idea of settling at the falls. Again nothing came of his efforts, and again he started for Jamestown.

On that last return trip to the settlement, John Smith was asleep in his boat one night when his powder bag was accidentally fired by someone. In the searing explosion that followed, the Captain was so badly burned that, momentarily crazed by the torment of pain, he leaped overboard into the deep river and almost drowned. With nothing to relieve his terrible suffering, he was brought the seventy remaining miles back to the fort.

All was bedlam here and the meagre store of provisions was diminishing daily with no replenishments.

Smith's old enemies returned to the attack and he was deposed from his office. In his weakened and disabled condition the situation was more than even the stout-hearted Captain could cope with. On October 4, 1609, he sailed for England aboard one of Somers's ships that had reached Jamestown after surviving the hurricane.

Captain John Smith was only twenty-nine years old when he left Virginia never to return, but he was like an old lion licking his wounds, of both the flesh and the spirit, on that day when he took final leave of the colony to which he had given such heroic service. But John Smith lived to add another memorable chapter to the history of his American explorations and discoveries. In 1614 he made such a thorough survey of that area of America which he named New England that he has been called its founder. And he lived to write his own history of his experiences in Virginia and New England. Scholars turn to this history for authentic information about those early English efforts to gain a permanent foothold in the New World. John Smith was more than a swashbuckling soldier of fortune. Only a man of daring vision, rare courage and endowments of a high order could have achieved what this first great American accomplished in many fields.

CHAPTER XII   *The Colonists Starve*

As Captain John Smith's ship sailed out of Chesapeake Bay a little pinnace nosed in and turned its prow up the James. It was another of the hurricane stragglers belonging to Somers's fleet and its name was the *Virginia*. Up at Sagadahoc on the present coast of Maine an attempt at English settlement had been made a few months after the founding of Jamestown. It was another failure, but before these colonists abandoned Sagadahoc they built this sturdy little thirty-ton pinnace which carried some of them back to England and then set sail the following year with the Somers fleet. So here was the *Virginia*, the first ocean-going ship ever to be built in America by Englishmen, completing her second trip across the stormy Atlantic.

Again the settlers, old and new, flocked down to the bank of the river to watch a ship come in after her sails had been sighted. But now there were the strained, anxious faces of women among the watchers, and the wan faces of their underfed and sickly children. It was the *Sea Venture* that they looked and prayed for most hopefully, for more supplies and provisions had been stored on Somers's flagship than on any of the others. But this little vessel was not the *Sea Venture*—they knew that sometime before she anchored. "Where is the *Sea Venture?*" they vainly asked the weary passengers landing from the *Virginia*.

With approximately three hundred new arrivals from the seven ships that had finally reached Jamestown, the population of the colony had now increased to about five hundred and conditions were going from very bad to much worse. The three members of the old council who had returned on Somers's ships, and had finally deposed Captain Smith, set themselves up as a council-of-sorts with some of the men who had expected to hold office under Governor Gates. With the weak and ailing Captain George Percy as their president, they attempted to manage the tottering colony until further instructions came from the Council in London.

But there was no able leader to enforce the discipline and the cooperative effort which were necessary to avert disaster. No leader strong enough to put fear and respect in the savages who, having quickly learned of Captain Smith's departure, were now on the warpath in open revolt. Powhatan no longer made any pretense of friendship for the English colonists. His subjects came no more to the fort with gifts of corn and venison and wild turkeys. "We now had nothing from them but mortal wounds with clubs and arrows," the desperate settlers cried.

Captain John Martin and Mr. Francis West finally got back to Jamestown after having lost most of their boats and half their men in savage encounters with the natives. Upon his return from Point Comfort, where he had built Algernon Fort, Captain John Ratcliffe set forth in a pinnace with some thirty or forty men to trade for corn in Powhatan's country. And that was the end of John Smith's old enemy who had clamored to have him hanged. He and most of his men were slain by the old chieftain's warriors. Mr. Francis West, who had also gone foraging among the Indians about the same time, fared better. He escaped the savages' deadly arrows but he brought back no corn and he did not return to Jamestown. Instead he turned the prow of his pinnace eastward and sailed for England.

In London Mr. West found his brother Lord Delaware and the other members of the Council wrestling with the problem of how to raise the necessary funds for the expedition they had expected to launch in August. After the excitement of the campaign for subscriptions to the joint-stock died down, many subscribers regretted they had bought the stock and lagged in their payments, or didn't pay at all.

Reports that reached London that fall of 1609 of the disappearance of the *Sea Venture*, and with it Somers, Gates and Newport, and of the confusion and misery in the colony did nothing to restore enthusiasm and boost stocks. So the Company finally told the people bluntly, in circulars distributed far and wide, that this was something they had to face as a moral duty—that if Englishmen were willing to risk their lives in such a venture the least they could do was to risk their money. The admonition worked—but even so, Lord Delaware could not get away before spring.

And most of the planters and their wives and children who had embarked so hopefully on a new life in a new land far from England's shores, never saw the beauty of that flowering spring of 1610 in Virginia, or any other.

As the leaves of a brilliant autumn turned brown, then shriveled and fell, the bleakness of another winter was more than matched by the bleakness of the lives of the people who struggled desperately for existence in the overcrowded settlement at Jamestown. Those who had not sickened and died of some disease, starved to death, or been fatally pierced by an Indian's arrow, no longer went down to the gray river's bank to look hopefully downstream for the white sails of the *Sea Venture*. The *Sea Venture* had become a phantom ship and they saw her only as a kind of mirage in fitful sleep. During their waking hours they thought of nothing and struggled for nothing except what had become the two terrible, stark necessities of life itself—food and warmth.

As the cutting winds whined through the bare branches and sleety rains fell, they began hacking away at the fort for firewood. Famished and ill, they were too weak to cut down the big trees—the oak and the walnut and the chestnut and the elm—that grew all around them. And those who were able were afraid to venture into the wilderness for brushwood for fear of Indian arrows. So they chopped up the palisades and when the gates of the fort fell from their hinges they lugged them off to feed the fires in their miserable houses that were falling down, too.

The savages made raids on their hogs down on Hog Island and within a short time not a squeal or a grunt could be heard down there. The chickens and goats and sheep and horses were quickly devoured. Then there was nothing to be had from the common store except the eight ounces of meal and the half pint of peas, squirmy with maggots, that was rationed out to each person once a day as long as these scant provisions lasted. The woods, as far as they dared go, were scoured for acorns, herbs, berries, roots, bark—for anything that could be chewed up and swallowed. And finally the few starved survivors hunted for rats, snakes and toadstools.

Not all the desperate men at Jamestown waited patiently for death to relieve their wretchedness as the terrible winter and spring of 1610 wore on. Some became deserters and threw themselves upon the mercy of the Indians to whose villages they fled. If recaptured by those who grimly tried to maintain some discipline, they were promptly hanged, shot or broken upon the wheel. Others were driven by gnawing hunger to steal from the common store as long as there was any food left. The poor wretch who one day was caught making away with a few pints of wormy oatmeal was taught never to steal again. A bodkin was thrust through his tongue and then he was chained to a tree where he was left to die of starvation. And there were those who found just the effort to live—by foraging, running away, or stealing—to be too much. They slipped quietly away unnoticed and dug holes deep enough in the earth to hide themselves in and there quietly starved to death.

Of the five hundred people who were swarming over the little settlement in the fall of 1609, not more than sixty were alive in May of 1610 to see the white lilies that bloomed in the gardens and the wild mallows that flaunted their red-purple blossoms in the deep-green woods. And, nearer dead than alive, these pitiful few were insensitive to the fragrance and the bright beauty of that fair spring. They were the survivors of what came to be called the Starving Time.

It was not just starvation, however, that had caused the deaths of all the others, and of many who had died at other times, presumably for the same reason. In outfitting the expeditions, the adventurers tried to make adequate provision for the departing settlers until their first harvest. But too often the supplies were insufficient for lack of funds. Frequently the ships were delayed in sailing and the colonists arrived too late to plant the seeds they had brought that year. And they landed in a weakened physical condition. The voyages were long, very long when hurricanes struck, and the ships were overcrowded. The diet was not well-balanced and toward the end of the voyage the food was rancid and the water stale.

Some of the passengers were already suffering from scurvy and malnutrition when they got off the ships.

Few of them had the strength to resist the diseases that plagued the swampy island they had come to—the malaria, the ague, the dysentery. And contagion and misery were spread when large numbers of newcomers overcrowded the settlement.

Help from the improvident natives was limited and unpredictable, and few of the settlers from England's towns and cities were experienced enough as woodsmen to live, as the Indians could, on what nature provided. Even if they had been, hunting and fishing were always hazardous because of the ever-lurking savages. And finally, there were always too many loafers and shirkers. So for these reasons, in a time of crisis, especially when there was confusion and the lack of a strong leader, those who were not wiped out by the Indians sickened and died, or starved to death.

CHAPTER XIII   *Governor Gates Brings*
News of the Sea Venture

DOWN AT POINT COMFORT a few men under the command of Captain James Davis had kept guard at Algernon Fort. And here Captain George Percy came one day to talk to Captain Davis about his plan of trying to save some of the starving settlers by moving them down to the fort. In the midst of their talk they were suddenly startled by a shout from the watch-tower. "Captain! Captain! Ships! Two ships are coming into the bay!"

Every man in the fort, along with Captain Davis and Captain Percy, ran to look out over the waters. It had been so long since the last ship had come through the great gateway of the capes that they had almost given up hope of help ever coming again from abroad. But were these ships, hardly more than white blobs in the far distance, manned by enemy or friend? There was no way of telling, though the men strained their eyes to see what kinds of vessels they might be. Captain Davis was suspicious rather than hopeful. The Spanish had threatened many times to wipe out the English settlement at Jamestown, and the little fort here at Point Comfort had been built as an outpost for the protection of the colony. No risks should be taken, so Captain Davis ordered every man on guard that night.

The captains of those two ships sailing into Chesapeake Bay did not know either whether fellow-countrymen or enemies occupied the strange fort they could see in the distance. They approached warily, as fearful as those watching them of attack. But the next morning after much signaling and counter-signaling, it became clear that all was well—that Englishmen were again coming across the waters of the Chesapeake to greet Englishmen on the western shores!

And those who watched, eagerly now, and waited, began to wonder again, but without fear. Who could they be? The ships came steadily closer with white sails spread. Passengers crowded the decks, among them women and children—and a tall figure that towered above all the rest in the lead boat.

"Sir Thomas Gates!" Captain George Percy suddenly cried.

And a chorus of shouts went up from the men who stood by. "The *Sea Venture!* The *Sea Venture!*"

The first Governor of the Colony of Virginia had, indeed, arrived at long last, and with him Admiral Somers, Vice-Admiral Newport and one hundred and forty passengers who had sailed on the *Sea Venture*. But they had not reached their destination, after so many months, aboard their flagship. That was the story they had to tell. That was the story the men at Algernon Fort were clamoring to hear almost before Governor Gates, and as many of his fellow-passengers as the fort could accommodate, had disembarked. For, as the boats came near and anchored, those who watched had seen what they had been too excited to realize before: that neither of these small pinnaces could be the great flagship of the fleet. *What* had happened to the *Sea Venture?*

But it was the tall, bearded Governor who asked the first question. In truth, he shot that question at Captain Percy the moment their hands clasped in greeting and welcome. "What can you tell me of the other ships of our fleet—have they arrived yet?"

And Captain George Percy quickly answered, "Sir, by God's mercy, seven of your ships have already passed through these capes and anchored at Jamestown."

"Thank God!" the Governor said fervently.

But Captain Percy was not yet ready to tell Sir Thomas of the sad fate that had befallen so many of the colonists who had landed from those seven ships. That would have to be told later. First he and the men at the fort must have the news of the *Sea Venture* for which they had waited so long.

Governor Gates himself began the dramatic story

[137]

after the company had assembled inside the fort. "It was a doomed ship we rode during those terrible days and nights of the hurricane," he said heavily, as though still under the weight of terror they had all felt. "You have surely heard from those who arrived ahead of us what a fearful storm it was. Never were ships given a more savage battering by howling winds and roaring waves than ours. We were towing our smallest ship, the *Catch*, when the hurricane struck, and soon the towline broke. The little boat was quickly swallowed up, with all on board, by the tumultuous waves—lost, every one of them. Then the next day all we could see of the other ships were their stark masts leaning crazily in the gloom. The raging storm drove us farther and farther apart until we could see nothing except the mountainous waves of that angry, heaving sea all around us."

The Governor paused, and for a moment silence lay upon the group. In silence every man and woman present felt the wordless terror of that awesome experience.

The gruff voice of the old Admiral broke the spell. "That wasn't all," he said solemnly. "In the very beginning the *Sea Venture* sprang a mighty leak, and here we were about to be drowned like rats within while we stood looking up and expecting death from the flood pouring down upon us from above. The ship was suddenly five feet deep in water above her ballast, and we had every man busy either bailing and pumping out the water or searching the ship from end to end for leaks, for it began to look as though she was cracking apart in every rib and seam."

"What a sight!" Secretary William Strachey exclaimed. "An eerie sight it was. The master, the master's mate, the boatswain, the quarter-master and the coopers and the carpenters creeping and poking about that rocking ship, holding up flickering candles to look into every corner and listen in every place for the water that was running in. The leaks they plugged!"

"And during all this time," young Captain George Yeardley added, "the heavens were so black we could not see a star by night, and by day nothing but a kind of ghostly light that filtered through the murk!"

"Oh, no," Admiral Somers interrupted with a gleam in his steel-gray eyes, "you forget, young man, that Thursday night when I was on watch! That was the night I saw the apparition of a little round light, like a faint star, that came streaming out of the blackness in a sparkling blaze. It perched half-way up the topmast and there paused and trembled for a moment before shooting off to one of the mast lines. After that it was a dancing star for three or four hours that leaped from one rope to another."

"What we all know as St. Elmo's fire, a light caused by atmospheric electricity," William Strachey explained, "but in that storm on that black night it looked like a trick the devil himself was playing on us."

Vice-Admiral Christopher Newport now spoke up quietly for the first time. "And it was our Admiral who first sighted and cried land when no man aboard dreamed of such happiness."

"Yes, yes," Secretary Strachey said excitedly, "the storm had abated and our unbelieving eyes made out, some distance ahead, the movement of trees swayed by the wind. And presently our gallant flagship, battered and waterlogged, was driven aground between two huge rocks just off the Bermuda Isles."

"Ah, the Bermudas!" several of the newcomers sighed longingly as they looked about the rough fort and out over the wide waters of the Chesapeake.

"The *Sea Venture* was a doomed ship," Secretary Strachey continued, "but by God's providential care not a passenger was lost. All of us reached one of the islands safely and later salvaged much of our equipment and most of our provisions."

An enchanted island it had seemed to them. Beyond the coral strand the sun shone dazzlingly out of a deep-blue sky upon a green island of lush beauty. Red, green and yellow birds flashed through the branches of strange trees, and everywhere there was the brilliant color of exotic plants blooming and growing in luxuriant profusion. They found the climate mild and healthful, and food was plentiful. Citrus fruits grew wild, there were groves of date and coconut palms, the waters teemed with fish. And many years earlier some Spanish sailors had loosed a number of hogs on the island. These swine had multiplied at such a rate that the island on which the English castaways had landed was overrun with them. With the help of a good hunting dog that they had brought along, the Englishmen had sometimes returned to the settlement from a hunting expedition with as many as fifty live boars, sows and pigs. And so they had lived here for almost a year in ease and comfort and plenty, knowing nothing of the fate of the seven other ships that had sailed with the *Sea Venture*.

"But we did not become lotus-eaters, content to spend the rest of our lives in this paradise," Governor Gates hastened to add after various members of the company had described the beauties and delights of the fair Bermuda island. "We had a mission to complete, and our men were soon building from the timber of the pungent Bermuda cedars and parts of our wrecked ship the two pinnaces that brought us here. One we named the *Deliverance* and the other the *Patience*."

Admiral Somers told of the effort they had made to send word of their fate to Jamestown. The long boat had been salvaged from the *Sea Venture*, and soon after their arrival in the Bermudas, Master's Mate Henry Ravens had rowed away with Cape Merchant Thomas Whittingham and six sailors bound for the Virginia settlement. They were never seen again, though beacons had been kept burning upon a Bermudian promontory for two moons.

And so the months had passed. The wedding of Thomas Powell and Elizabeth Parsons had been celebrated in the strange, beautiful land of Bermuda. A baby boy had been born to Master and Mistress Edward Eason. Mistress Eason was on board one of the pinnaces at that very moment holding little Bermudas Eason. But little Bermuda Rolfe, the baby daughter of Master and Mistress John Rolfe who had also been born on the island refuge, did not live to come to Virginia with her parents. Her tiny grave was back there on the green island among those of several adults who also had died.

The long, exciting story had been told. At last those who had watched and waited at Algernon Fort knew what had happened to the *Sea Venture* and her passengers.

CHAPTER XIV   *James Fort Is Abandoned*

AND NOW JAMESTOWN—what was the news of the
little settlement that was to be home to these colonists
who had been so long on their perilous way from the
mother country? The new arrivals, fresh and hearty
after months of good living in the Bermudas, asked Captain George Percy this question with hopeful eagerness.
And Captain Percy had to tell them that most of the
settlers they had expected to see there were dead, that
famine threatened the few who were still alive and that
the town itself was in ruins.

The men and women gathered around the Captain
heard the news in stunned silence. Then the heavy sinking of the heart as it had been with those who had arrived ahead of them. Most of them forgot the high-
hearted purposes for which they had sacrificed so
much to come to this far country and wished they had

never left England—or Bermuda. But, bad as the out-look was, this was no time for indecision and looking backward.

Responsibility now rested upon Governor Gates, and with a deeply troubled look upon his rugged face, he ordered the *Deliverance* and the *Patience* to proceed without delay up the James. With no ripple of wind and only the tides to help them, it was two days before the ships anchored at Jamestown.

There was no glad hail for the newcomers from the river bank—no excited crowd waiting to give them a joyous welcome. There was nothing but misery in the faces of the little group of men and women who had come down to the landing when they saw the ships approaching. Here was help at last, but they were too weak for excitement when they learned it was their Governor who had come and with him the colonists who had sailed on the *Sea Venture* and been given up for lost.

Governor Gates was visibly shocked by the ram-shackle appearance of the town, but the forlorn little chapel still stood, so he commanded the bell to be rung to call all who were able to come to prayer. It was like a bell that tolled, so sad was the procession that followed the new minister, the Reverend Richard Buck, into the house of worship. And the minister's prayer was sor-rowful. Everyone's heart was too heavy and sad for joyous praise and thanksgiving. God must have under-stood.

But it was not a time to give way to grief and despair. Nor was there any time to lose. Governor Gates made his decision quickly. No matter what the adventurers in London thought, Jamestown had to be abandoned and its people returned to England before they starved to death. There was food enough on the *Deliverance* and the *Patience* for immediate relief, but beyond that there was nothing but the serious threat of starvation.

Besides the two pinnaces in which the colonists had come from Bermuda, there were the *Virginia* and the *Discovery* at Jamestown. Into these four small ships two hundred people would have to be crowded, but it could be done. All able-bodied men were set to work making pitch and tar for the boats, the women baked bread and the meager personal possessions were hastily bundled.

There were some who urged the Governor to burn the town, but this Sir Thomas Gates would not do. To prevent it, he ordered Captain George Yeardley to keep a watchful eye on the settlement while preparations for an orderly embarkation went forward.

All was ready on June 7th for the final leave-taking. The *Virginia* had been sent ahead to Algernon Fort to pick up Captain Davis and his men. Everything of value had been loaded on the ships and the heavy ordnance had been buried in front of the fort's main gate. All morning the Governor had been busy overseeing last-minute activities. And now he stood beside the entrance to the fort. At his command the drummer gave the signal for every man and woman who still lingered to go aboard ship. And presently the tall figure of Governor Gates was striding down the road to the landing —the last man to leave the island.

About noon a sad farewell salute was fired with small arms and the little fleet turned eastward and dropped down the James. That night the tide carried them as far as Hog Island and the next morning they reached Mulberry Island. And here they met the *Virginia!* Why had the *Virginia,* which was to have joined them at Algernon Fort, come back? The mystified colonists saw a young man salute the Governor and hand him a letter. What could it mean? There was excitement now and the babble of conjecture among the passengers as each one gave his or her opinion as to what might be afoot.

Finally the electrifying word of explanation went round. The young man was Captain Edward Brewster and he had brought Governor Gates a message from none other than Lord Delaware himself! Lord Delaware, Governor and Captain-General of Virginia, was off Point Comfort with three ships and one hundred and fifty colonists! Sir Thomas Gates, who had filled the office for his Lordship for so short a time, was no longer governor.

After the bewildered settlers had recovered from this startling news the excited talk broke out afresh. What would they do now? What would be his Lordship's orders? And presently they learned, to their grief and consternation, that they had been ordered back to the dismal settlement they had so recently left—forever, all of them had hoped.

So the three pinnaces—the *Discovery*, the *Deliverance* and the *Patience*—swung round and started back to Jamestown. Ex-Governor Gates boarded the *Virginia* and proceeded downstream with all possible speed to welcome his Lordship.

On Sunday, June 10, 1610, Lord Delaware arrived at Jamestown with his new planters, fresh from England. Sir Thomas had told him of the wretched state of the settlement. He had also told him of the recent arrival of the survivors, including himself, of the wrecked *Sea Venture*. "But for this happy news," his Lordship declared, "the lamentable condition of the colony would have been sufficient to have broken my heart and to have made me altogether unable to have done my King and country any service."

But the Lord Governor did not falter. For all the disastrous happenings, he saw in the crumbling and despairing little colony the beginnings of a new nation. And prestige and authority were, in his opinion, very important in lifting it out of the doldrums. Others must already have known what was expected of them, for Captain George Yeardley was at the landing when the new Governor arrived with his company drawn up in ceremonious formation, with Secretary William Strachey acting as color-bearer.

Lord Delaware's first act upon setting foot on Virginia soil was to drop to his knees and, in the midst of the assembled company who stood with bowed heads, offer up a long and silent prayer to God. Then he arose and strode solemnly into the town with Secretary Strachey leading the way and making sweeping bows at intervals as he dipped the color standard. The Governor and his party, followed by the crowd of men and women, went at once to the shabby little chapel where the Reverend Richard Buck awaited their coming.

The sermon the Jamestown settlers heard that day was not in the sad, sorrowful key of the first service the Reverend Buck had conducted upon his and Sir Thomas Gates's arrival a few days earlier. Praise and thanksgiving and hope were its triumphant notes. For God's hand was clearly seen in the successive events that had saved Jamestown. Sir Thomas Gates and Sir George Somers along with the *Sea Venture's* passengers had not perished in the hurricane. The Bermudas had preserved them and they had arrived at the settlement at a critical hour. Sir Thomas Gates had not permitted the fort to be burned when it was abandoned. Lord Delaware had come with fresh hope, fresh colonists and a year's provisions and supplies, but if Sir Thomas had set sail sooner he probably would never have met him on the vast ocean! "Never had any people more just cause to cast themselves at the very foot-stool of God and to revere his mercy than this distressed colony." That was the theme of the Reverend Richard Buck's sermon in Jamestown on Sunday, June 10, 1610.

And among all the good works the Lord Governor started the first was the restoration of the church. A chancel of cedar was built and a beautiful communion table of black walnut. The pews and the pulpit were of fragrant cedar, too, and the windows were made broad so that air and sunlight could fill and brighten the house of God. And two deep-toned bells were hung in the steeple.

It was the Lord Governor's idea, too, that flowers would make the church more beautiful. So the ladies of Jamestown brought English blossoms from their small garden plots and sprays of the wild-blooming honeysuckle and red-bud in the spring, and in the autumn the scarlet glory of the turning leaves. Perhaps a lovely girl named Temperance Flowerdew helped with the decoration. She had come to Jamestown with the colonists from Bermuda and some years later became the bride of Captain George Yeardley. Their romance may have blossomed in the bright, cedar-fragrant chapel, for services were a matter of twice-daily attendance that was compulsory. Then there was the elaborate Sunday ceremony when the Lord Governor came in regal state accompanied by all the members of his advisory council, all the captains and other officers and with a guard of fifty halberdiers dressed in rich red cloaks. He sat in the choir on a chair upholstered in green velvet and at his feet was a green velvet cushion upon which he knelt.

Inspired by new courage and new resolution and a deep faith, the Jamestown adventure carried on.

CHAPTER XV   *Samuel Argall Kidnaps*
Pocahontas

IN 1613 life at the plantation on the James was still hard and precarious. But the hardy survivors of all the misfortunes could now see the heartening results of their heroic labors. Like a plant or a tree faithfully tended, the roots of the little settlement had gone deeper and taken firmer hold in Virginia soil. And in that year of 1613 one of those momentous events happened that brought rare good fortune to the colony.

Lord Delaware had gone back to England. Within the year after his arrival at Jamestown in 1610, he had learned from personal experience how the colonists had to struggle to survive the diseases that afflicted them on

[150]

the swampy island. His Lordship was so exhausted at the end of the year by a succession of protracted ill-nesses—chills and fevers, dysentery and scurvy—that he was unable to carry on longer his duties as governor.

In spite of his long bouts with sickness the Lord Governor had accomplished much during that year. Discipline had been restored, the town had been cleaned up, sagging buildings had been repaired and new ones erected, and Forts Henry and Charles had been constructed down on the lower James as further protection for the settlement.

The good work went on under the firm hand of Sir Thomas Dale who came over as Lord Delaware's suc-cessor. Governor Dale was a stern disciplinarian but an able man. Gradually Jamestown became something more than just a huddle of buildings inside a fort. It be-came a real town. A town with just one street outside the triangular fort, but a street with two rows of framed timber houses two-stories-and-a-garret high. James-town was growing up! Quite a big storehouse had been built, too. It was one hundred twenty feet long and forty feet wide. But the colonists no longer had to de-pend entirely on the storehouse for subsistence. They now had their individual houses with gardens in which they raised their own vegetables—parsnips, carrots, tur-nips, pumpkins and melons. The ships no longer roped up to the big cypresses along the bank of the James—a real pier had been built! And the increasing numbers of cattle and horses that were being brought over found shelters that the industrious settlers had built in their growing town. There was even time for fun—the men bowled in the streets. Governor Dale thought they bowled too much.

But Governor Dale gave up the governorship for a time to undertake what the adventurers in London had long wanted—some more plantations, or seats. And during his absence from Jamestown, tall Sir Thomas Gates took over the duties of governor again.

Dale cruised up the James, and upon a high neck of land about twelve miles below the falls, chose a site for a town which he named Henrico in honor of Prince Henry. Three hundred colonists moved from Jamestown up to Henrico, and before long they had three streets of well-framed houses, a handsome church, a storehouse and some watch-houses. Then Bermuda City, later to be called Charles City, mushroomed on a favorable location some five miles distant by land from Henrico. And outside all these towns little isolated farm houses and individual plantations began to dot the island in brave defiance of the Indians. But there were block houses at strategic points, and Jamestown and Henrico and Bermuda City were palisaded towns. Stout cedar posts impaled them against Indian attack just as the fort was so protected.

During these years of expansion Captain Samuel Argall had taken an important and active part in the work of the colony. The same Captain Argall who had pioneered in finding a shorter route across the Atlantic and from whom the colonists had learned of the reorganization of the government in London. Like Captain John Smith he was a man of energy and initiative, and he had Smith's knack of getting along well with the natives. Since 1609 he had served the colony as an able successor to the Captain both in trading and in exploration.

Although the colonists were now raising a variety of vegetables in their own gardens, they still depended upon the Indians for additional supplies of corn. And the savages, particularly those under old Powhatan's rule, were still unfriendly. Captain Argall had ranged beyond Powhatan's territory and had opened up trade with the natives along the Potomac River—trade in furs as well as corn. Two small vessels were kept at Jamestown for this purpose and large supplies of copper trinkets, beads, hoes, knives, bells, scissors and hatchets that the savages valued so highly. In exchange Captain Argall often brought back rich stores of furs that were shipped to England—deerskins and the pelts of the wildcat, fox, beaver, otter and raccoon.

It was just another routine trading expedition for Captain Samuel Argall up in the Potomac territory in the spring of 1613 when he learned that Pocahontas, daughter of Powhatan, was there on a visit at the habitation of the werowance Japasaws. It must have been a flash of inspiration that gave him the idea of capturing her and holding her as a hostage. To trap her as he did was a cruel way to treat the lovely eighteen-year-old Indian girl who had so often, in times past, befriended and helped the Jamestown colonists. But it had unbelievably happy results for both Pocahontas and the colony.

The old Emperor had continued to cause trouble for the settlers, and he was now holding a number of Englishmen prisoners; and his braves had pilfered a quantity of guns, swords and tools from the settlement. Nothing had come of the colonists' complaints and demands that both the imprisoned men and the stolen goods be returned. So now Argall reasoned that with his beloved daughter held as a hostage the old Chief would act, and act fast, in settling this account.

Japasaws was an old friend of Captain John Smith, and it was most favorable to Captain Argall's plan that he was now his friend, too. And Japasaws' black eyes had caught the gleam of a shiny little copper kettle Argall had with him on this trip. So the Englishman worked swiftly. All that he needed was to get Pocahontas on his boat, but he needed his Indian friend's help to do that. "We'll treat her kindly, Japasaws," he said, after he had explained why he wanted her as a hostage. "No harm will come to her at Jamestown. Just help me to get her on my ship and in return for that I'll give you the copper kettle and some beads and hatchets, or anything else you want."

The shiny little copper kettle! Japasaws smiled, rubbed his hands, and said, "Yes." And then he went off to have a long talk with his wife, for the plan he and Argall made required her help, too.

And everything worked smoothly according to the plan. The wife said she wanted to see the English captain's ship. Japasaws pretended to be shocked. There were no women on the Captain's boat. He scolded her and she wept, feigning to be hurt by her husband's harsh words. Her tears seemed to make him feel sorry for her.

"If Pocahontas comes with you, maybe that will make it all right," he said.

So Japasaws and his wife and the unsuspecting Pocahontas came aboard Captain Argall's ship. After the Captain had shown them over the boat he led them into his cabin where a feast had been laid for his guests. During the meal Japasaws stepped often on his foot to remind him that he had done his part.

When the meal was finished Captain Argall persuaded Pocahontas to go to the gunroom while he had a little business talk with Japasaws. After he had rewarded his friend as he had promised, he sent for her and told her bluntly that she was his prisoner whom he was taking back to Jamestown to hold as a hostage there until her father returned the Englishmen and the stolen goods. Japasaws and his wife pretended to be deeply shocked and wailed loudly. But they were soon merrily on their way back to the werowance's seat with the kettle and the trinkets. And Pocahontas was presently on her way to Jamestown in the custody of Captain Samuel Argall.

It is quite likely that after the gentle Indian girl had ceased weeping she began to think of going back to Jamestown with pleasure. For she had not visited the settlement since Captain John Smith's departure in the fall of 1609. And during those years while her father waged a bitter fight against the English colonists no word was heard of her at the fort. She was left quietly to herself on the little ship, and as it sailed down the Chesapeake her thoughts must have been filled with memories of the days when she came often to the settlement with her wild Indian friends; of the days when she came with gifts of food for the hungry men; when she came fearlessly, light-footed as a fawn, through the deep woods in the dark of night to warn them of danger; when, as a laughing child, she turned cartwheels and somersaults in the market place. And her dear friend, Captain John Smith—was he dead as she had been told? Undoubtedly she thought of him and wondered, and saw him again in all the little memory-pictures she had of him.

But Pocahontas was no longer a child. There must have been the sad realization of this in her thoughts as she looked into the unknown future and tried to puzzle out what it might hold for her. She knew she had turned her last cartwheel in the market place of Jamestown. Now she was going back to the scenes of her childhood as a young woman with the grave responsibilities that come with growing up. The little Indian maiden knew she had grown up and that, at the moment, her future was dark and troubled.

CHAPTER XVI   *John Rolfe and Pocahontas Become Engaged*

So POCAHONTAS CAME BACK to Jamestown—not as a prisoner, really. No one would have known it, seeing her escorted off the boat as the Indian princess she was, daughter of the great chief Powhatan—seeing her introduced to Governor Gates who bent his tall figure to bow low over her small brown hand. Not even as the Indian girl she was, for coming back to Jamestown was like coming home to Pocahontas who had already learned to love the English people and their more civilized way of life, even in this rude settlement. Many, maybe most, of her old friends and acquaintances were dead. But no doubt she remembered the humble carpenter, John Laydon, who must have been there to welcome her and introduce her to his wife Anne and their little daughter Virginia, who had been born in 1609. There were, of course, many new faces that Pocahontas had never seen before, among them that of the Reverend Alexander Whitaker.

The Reverend Alexander Whitaker had come to Virginia as assistant to the Reverend Richard Buck, and it was to his home that Pocahontas was taken upon her arrival in Jamestown. Here she was treated by the minister and his wife as an honored guest and shown every kindness and consideration. And in this atmosphere of love and kindness and thoughtfulness the Indian girl responded to the gentle teachings of a new and different religion.

Under the kindly instruction of her custodian, the Reverend Alexander Whitaker, Pocahontas came to know a great teacher she had never known before—Jesus Christ. She came to know God, too, as Christians knew Him. Twice each day she went with the women of Jamestown to prayers in the little chapel, and twice each Sunday she went to the services conducted by the Reverend Richard Buck and the Reverend Alexander Whitaker.

A message had been sent to Powhatan following the arrival of his daughter in Jamestown that informed him of the situation. He was assured that Pocahontas would be well treated, but that she would be kept until he ransomed her with the English prisoners and the stolen arms and tools.

It was three months before the old Emperor, who professed to love this daughter so dearly, deigned to take notice of the communication. Then he grudgingly returned the seven Englishmen he had held prisoners but said the arms and tools had been stolen from him and were now scattered beyond recovery. This did not please the authorities at Jamestown. They thanked him for the return of the prisoners but firmly demanded that he do something about the pilfered goods. They also suggested that it was about time he made peace with them. And there the matter stood for some months longer.

Meanwhile Pocahontas made such progress in her study of the Christian religion that the day came when, by her own wish, she was ready to renounce the gods of her own people. There was a beautiful ceremony in the little chapel at which she confessed her faith in Jesus Christ and the Christian God. And in her baptism in a new faith she was given a new name. Pocahontas, the Church of England's first convert among the native Virginians, was christened "Rebecca."

So the young Indian princess who would always be known to the world as Pocahontas now had three names. For her first and real name was Matoaka. That name had been concealed from the English by her people because of the superstitious fear that if it were known harm would come to them.

During this momentous year while she was held as a hostage in Jamestown, Pocahontas had yet another deeply moving experience. She fell in love. She fell in love with a young Englishman named John Rolfe and he returned that love with such deep feeling that the barrier of her wild race was no barrier at all to him.

John Rolfe was an educated English gentleman from

a fine old English family. He and his wife had been passengers on the *Sea Venture,* and their one child had been born and buried on the Bermuda island where they had lived for a time with the other castaways of the wrecked ship. Soon after their arrival in Jamestown John Rolfe's wife had died, and the one interest in the young planter's life after that had been tobacco. Until that memorable year when Pocahontas came. John Rolfe went right on cultivating the bitter-leaved little Virginia plant that was to bring wealth and security to the Virginia plantations—but he also began to cultivate the love of the Indian princess who had stirred his own heart to love again.

In the spring of 1614 Governor Gates returned to England and Sir Thomas Dale again took over the duties of governor in Jamestown. And the first thing he did was to outfit an expedition to sail up the York to settle matters with Powhatan in person. About one hundred and fifty armed men accompanied him, and on his own ship, the *Treasurer,* were Pocahontas and John Rolfe and Rolfe's good friend, Captain Ralph Hamor.

It was an exciting voyage. All along the way there were numerous encounters and peace talks with the embattled savages. At one point a werowance angrily threatened total destruction of the English colony, reminding Governor Dale of the fate that had befallen Captain Ratcliffe and his men. But Governor Thomas Dale was not a man to be easily intimidated, even by a savage chieftain. He replied that this treacherous attack on Englishmen was just cause for destroying Powhatan and all his people, as he intended to do if the old Emperor did not soon make peace. High up the river the English did land and kill some of the Indian warriors and burn their habitations, but Powhatan himself could not be reached for the conference Dale wanted with him.

Two of the old Chief's sons, more peaceably inclined than he, came aboard Governor Dale's ship, however, to greet their sister and marvel at how well she had been treated. They left promising to plead with their father to make peace with the English.

Time for the spring planting at the settlement was near now so Governor Dale prepared to turn his ships homeward. But before he left Powhatan's country he sent the Emperor word that if a satisfactory peace had not been concluded by harvest time the English would begin a relentless war on his people. And before the ships sailed down the York, Captain Ralph Hamor handed the governor a letter which took a long time to read because it was two thousand words long!

The letter was from John Rolfe, and in it the young planter made a full confession to Governor Dale of his love for the Indian girl, Pocahontas. He also revealed what torment and agitation he had suffered, fearing that it was wrong to love one of a heathen race. But his heart was so deeply entangled and enthralled, he confessed, that he could not free himself from this love. And then the light had come, it seemed to him, when he convinced himself that this marriage would be for the good of the plantation, for the honor of his country, for the glory of God and for his own salvation. And so it was— all of that. And wise Sir Thomas Dale must have known it would be, for in less time than it had taken him to read the letter he had given the young couple his blessing.

Before the *Treasurer* sailed, Pocahontas herself stepped ashore to announce the happy news of her betrothal to her brothers and a few of her father's chief men. Then she added, "You can tell my father that if he loved me he would not value me less than those old swords and axes. Therefore I shall go back and live with the English people who love me." Pocahontas had renounced more than the idolatry of the gods of her people!

There was merry-making and loud rejoicing on the ships that sailed back to Jamestown. The fighting and the parleying were forgotten in the joyous celebration of the forthcoming marriage of the Indian princess and a first citizen of Jamestown. And as the *Treasurer* sailed up the James with the red cross of St. George flying from her masthead, the guns boomed and the drums and the trumpets blared the glad news to all of Jamestown and the surrounding plantations. Perhaps the men and the women who flocked down to the wharf waving their arms wildly in happy welcome knew beforehand what their Governor's announcement would be. Certainly nobody could have been surprised.

CHAPTER XVII   *Wedding Bells Ring*

AND SO THERE WAS A WEDDING IN JAMESTOWN—the
most important wedding that had ever been solemnized
in the little chapel there. Such a wedding as was never
solemnized anywhere, before or since.

Happy days followed during the short time before
the nuptials for the little Indian bride-to-be and the
women of the colony. No doubt Pocahontas was already accustomed to the more civilized way of dressing
in the style of the English women of that early day.
And no doubt Temperance Flowerdew and Mistress
Forrest and Mistress Eason ransacked their wardrobes
and stitched far into the night by candlelight helping
her to get ready a proper trousseau for the bride of an

English gentleman. No record has been left of what the bride wore on her wedding day, but most likely she was dressed in a simple white gown, long and very full, and with a wreath of white flowers holding in place the filmy veil that fell from her black hair.

On April 5, 1614, the little church at Jamestown was filled to capacity by those who had assembled to witness the marriage of Pocahontas and John Rolfe—sailors and soldiers and colonists and Indians. The broad windows were opened wide to the beauty of still another blossoming spring. And inside, the chapel itself was like a woodland glade—wild flowers in profusion and everywhere branches and vines and ferns in the deep and tender greens of a new spring.

As the Reverend Richard Buck rose to stand before the altar in his long, flowing vestments and the flutes released their high, sweet notes that were warbled back by the birds outside, all eyes turned toward the door through which the lovely Pocahontas entered on the arm of her old uncle Apachisco. Turned and watched them walk slowly up the aisle—the dark-skinned, black-haired Indian girl in her white wedding gown and the swarthy, graying old uncle in his warrior's skins and feathers and beads.

At the altar Apachisco gave the bride to her groom. There by her Christian name of Rebecca the Reverend Richard Buck united her in marriage to John Rolfe according to the ritual of the Church of England.

And nothing but good came of this beautiful marriage which was a true union of a man and a woman deeply in love with each other. Though Powhatan was not at the wedding, he had sent the old uncle to act as his deputy and to give his daughter to the Englishman. He had also sent two of her brothers who were present at the ceremony. And at last the old Emperor's heart really softened toward the paleface intruders. The marriage of his daughter to one of them accomplished what all the strategy and warring and parleying had failed to do. As long thereafter as Powhatan lived there was peace between the Virginia colonists and his people. Terms of peace were also concluded with the Chickahominies, and there followed a period of such welfare and peace and prosperity for the settlers as had hitherto been unknown.

The young couple went to live in a plantation home John Rolfe had built on the James River near Henrico, and here their little son was born. He was named Thomas in honor of their good friend Sir Thomas Dale.

In June, 1616, the Rolfes with their infant son accompanied Sir Thomas to England. Here in the great halls of the nobility the little Indian girl who had grown to young womanhood in the Virginia wilderness was toasted and honored as the Lady Rebecca. Dressed in the elegant fashion of the English ladies of that day, she was entertained with pomp and ceremony by the Lord Bishop of London, and Lord and Lady Delaware presented her at Court.

Pocahontas assumed and played her role as a great lady in English Court circles with the dignity and grace becoming the daughter of a King. But there is no doubt that the experience which was most real to her, and that which really moved her gentle heart, was her meeting with the loved friend of her childhood whom she had thought to be dead. She was so overcome by emotion when she saw Captain John Smith for the first time during her London visit that she covered her face with her hands and it was some minutes before she could speak. Then she said, "They did tell me always that you were dead and I knew naught else until I came to Plymouth."

Pocahontas never saw her homeland again. In the month of March, 1617, she left London with her husband and son to board a ship at Gravesend that was to carry them back to Virginia. But on the eve of sailing she was stricken with a fatal illness. Knowing that death was near, she said quietly to her husband, "All must die —it is enough that our child liveth."

And the child, Thomas Rolfe, lived to become the ancestor of many distinguished Virginians.

CHAPTER XVIII *The First Representative*
Assembly Meets

JOHN ROLFE SHOULD BE RECOGNIZED and remembered for something more than his marriage to the Indian princess, Pocahontas. This marriage brought a long period of peace with the Indians which was a very great boon, indeed, to the harried colonists. But John Rolfe made still another contribution to the life and growth of the Virginia colony which entitles him to a place of outstanding importance in his own right.

American tobacco had been introduced to England back in the sixteenth century by Governor Ralph Lane of the ill-fated Roanoke Island colony. But English smokers did not like it because of its bitter taste. They preferred the tobacco which the Spanish exported from the West Indies. Why couldn't the sweet-tasting kind be produced on Virginia soil?

This problem intrigued the young planter, John Rolfe, and soon after his arrival in Jamestown he began quietly experimenting with the bitter-leaved Virginia product and with seeds from Trinidad and Venezuela. In time he succeeded in cultivating and curing tobacco of such excellence that there was immediate demand for it in England.

At last a profitable commodity had been discovered and developed that brought prosperity not only to the Jamestown settlement, but to all of Tidewater Virginia where great tobacco plantations were flourishing by the end of the seventeenth century. The short route to the South Sea was never discovered, nor the fabulous gold mines that had been the first lure of Virginia settlement. And such industrial enterprises as ironworks and salt works and the production of silk, oil, wine and hemp did not prove successful. But to John Rolfe is due the credit for having developed, by his own efforts, a product which gave profitable employment to shippers, merchants, manufacturers, farmers and laborers, and thereby laid the economic foundation of a new nation.

Early in October of the year 1616 the *Susan* anchored at the Jamestown wharf with a cargo of manufactured articles for which the Virginia planters paid in tobacco. And thereafter there was a regular exchange of goods between the colonists and the merchants of England.

In the meantime events of far-reaching importance were taking place within the council chambers of the Virginia Company in London. So important were they that the result was to be an achievement without precedent in the history of colonization; so important that the result has been recorded as one of the most notable events in American history.

In 1612 a new charter had been granted to the Virginia Company to replace that of 1609. Under the terms of the Charter of 1612 the officials and members of the Company were granted powers and privileges such as they had not had before. They began holding meetings four times a year which were called the Quarter Courts. These quarterly meetings were really legislative assemblies with political privileges much like those exercised by the King and Parliament.

Among the officials of the Virginia Company at this time were men with liberal ideas. And the outstanding leader among them was Sir Edwin Sandys. He believed in the rights of the people and in representative government. No man was more deeply interested in the welfare of the Virginia colonists than this great liberal, and he came to the conclusion that what the colony needed was not a change of governors but a change of government. What was more, he had the courage to work for something that had never been tried before. And because Sir Edwin Sandys was an influential member of the Company and was respected and liked by all the others, he succeeded in his revolutionary and ambitious plan of introducing popular government in Virginia.

The name the liberal leaders of the Virginia Company gave their plan was "the greate Charter of privileges, orders and laws." This famous document was drawn up sometime before November, 1618. And in its lengthy provisions that dealt with all aspects of life in the colony it was like a written constitution.

The great Charter provided for new land policies that would attract more and better colonists to Virginia. All adventurers and all the planters who had arrived before Governor Dale's departure in 1616 and who had settled at their own expense were given liberal rent-free grants of land. Those who had come over at the Company's expense were given the same amount at the end of seven years of service. Settlers who emigrated at the Company's expense after 1616 were free to dispose of their labor after a seven-year term as half-share tenants but were given no land grants. Then there was the famous headright provision of the Charter. It provided for a grant of fifty acres, on both a first and second dividend, for every person whose transportation to the colony was paid before the end of a seven-year period in 1625. Thus a man could acquire considerable acreage by transporting a number of persons at his own expense.

The headright outlasted the seven-year term and became the basis of Virginia's subsequent land policy. There was profit in paying the transportation of indentured servants and, later, of Negro slaves, and this in turn served the colony in helping it to meet its increasing need of labor. The indentured servant was one who sold his services, for the cost of his transportation, for a certain number of years, after which time he was free to live his life as he chose.

In 1617, Captain Samuel Argall, who was then governor of the colony, had fixed the boundaries of the four settlements large enough to be called towns. Designated as boroughs, these towns were James City (Jamestown), Charles City, Henrico and Kecoughtan. The revised land policies assigned three thousand acres in each borough as the Company's land that was to be cultivated by its tenants on a half-share basis. Land was also provided for the governor's support and for the minister's salary. Thus began early the American practice of setting aside land for public purposes.

The great Charter was ratified at a Quarter Court on November 28, 1618. The historic document was then handed over to the new governor, the young Captain who had become Sir George Yeardley. He sailed with it for Virginia the following January with instructions to call a general assembly of the planters soon after his arrival.

In April of 1619 Governor Yeardley issued the proclamation announcing that "the cruel laws by which we have so long been governed are now abrogated, and we are now governed by those free laws which his Majesty's subjects live under in England. And further, that liberty is now given to all men, to make the choice of their dividends of land and, as their abilities and means permit, to possess and plant upon them."

The Governor announced, too, that he had been given authority to call a general assembly once every year which was to consist of two members from each borough and each plantation. The burgesses, or representatives, were to be elected by the people—all the colonists except women and children and underage apprentices—and the governor and the council would meet with them in the general assembly.

And in late June the first elections were held. For the first time the people of this nation exercised the privilege of voting. It was an historic event when, by their free choice, the settlers of the eleven districts of the Virginia colony chose by ballot the twenty-two burgesses who were to represent them in their first general assembly.

It was in a very simple setting that one of the great scenes, perhaps the greatest, in the history of this country was enacted. The Governor, the council and the twenty-two burgesses met in the rude little wooden church in Jamestown on July 30, 1619. This was the first general assembly.

Led by Governor George Yeardley, the members of the first general assembly entered the church and took their places in the choir. The Governor sat in the seat he was accustomed to occupy at church services with the councilors ranged on either side. Directly in front of him was the speaker, John Pory, and beside him John Twine, the clerk. At the chair rail was Thomas Pierse, the sergeant, who was ready for any emergency. And round about them were the burgesses.

The meeting began with a prayer by the Reverend Richard Buck in which God's guidance was earnestly sought. Then all the members filed down into the body of the church. The councilors had already been sworn in, and now each burgess took the oath of allegiance to the King as his name was called.

With the preliminaries over, the assembly settled down to the important business for which it had been called. Speaker John Pory had already made a careful study of the great Charter of laws and privileges and had organized it into four main divisions which the various committees now took up for consideration. The burgesses were inexperienced as legislators, but they knew what their needs and problems as colonists were. So in a short time they had framed a number of new laws, made modifications of certain old laws and drawn up various petitions to the Company. At the very outset they exercised what is one of the fundamental human rights—the right of petition. One of their petitions requested that the laws they had made might become effective at once. And this request was granted them by the Company.

The assembly of 1619 lasted just six days, but the burgesses, inexperienced though they were, accomplished much in this short time and under difficult conditions. Virginia's summer climate had not changed! And during those hot, sticky days while they struggled with the problems of law-making Speaker Pory and many of the members suffered the usual summer indispositions, and one of the burgesses died. Before their first meeting adjourned they wisely decided to convene the following year on March 1st. During the closing sessions, too, provision for compensation to the speaker, the clerk, the sergeant and the provost marshal of

Jamestown was made by levying one pound of tobacco upon every man and man-servant above the age of sixteen.

And the burgesses felt a note of apology was due the Company for breaking up so suddenly after such a short session. They wrote an explanation of the situation, asked pardon for not having brought their work to greater perfection, and expressed the hope that the Company would accept their poor endeavor and in its wisdom be ready to support the weakness "of this little flock." The little flock had builded better than they knew in this first humble endeavor as legislators. They had, no less, laid the foundation itself of American democracy.

Two other events, of lesser importance but highly significant in the expanding life of the colony, rounded out the momentous year of 1619.

Far-sighted men in England who were deeply interested in the welfare of the Virginia colony saw clearly the need for women in the growing settlements in America where there were still far more men in the population. "Unless the settlers are provided with helpmates to make homes for them they will certainly return to England, as many have already done, after they have realized some profit from this venture," they reasoned.

No group was more sincerely and more actively interested in this problem than English clergymen. And it was due in large part to their efforts that young women were carefully selected in England who were willing to make the long voyage to a distant land on the high-hearted venture of finding a desirable husband there. The first contingent—ninety of them—came over during that memorable year of 1619. Provision for their care was made in the homes of married settlers and they were free to make their own choice of a husband or to remain single if they preferred. And the cost to the husbands who were chosen? One hundred and twenty pounds weight of the best leaf Virginia tobacco. John Rolfe's tobacco even bought wives in those days!

There was need, too, for more and more labor for the expanding tobacco plantations up and down the James that were soon to spread over all of Tidewater Virginia. At this time indentured servants met the demand, but the forerunners of a new source of labor supply arrived one day in September 1619 on board a ship that anchored at the Jamestown wharf. Whether on the *Treasurer* or a Dutch man-of-war is not known for certain. But for certain twenty-odd Negroes were escorted off a ship that day and sold for the provisions of food the ship that had brought them from the West Indies needed. They were not sold as slaves, however, and most, if not all, of them probably became free men in time. But their arrival can be said to have marked the beginning of the institution of slavery which some years later came to supply households and fields alike with black slave labor.

So it was that in this year of 1619 the roots of English colonization took deeper and firmer hold than ever before in the good earth of the New World. The critical tests had been met by venturer and adventurer alike "with a constant and patient resolution, until by the mercies of God" they had overcome them. The permanent success of the Jamestown adventure was at last assured.

CHAPTER XIX   *Bacon's Rebellion Dooms Jamestown*

JOHN PORY, who had served the first legislative assembly so well as its speaker, was now the colony's able secretary. In September of 1619 he wrote a long letter to the Virginia Company in which he gave a cheerful and optimistic report on the state of the settlement. There was abundance now from the sowing and the reaping. Abundance, too, of that peace and contentment in honest, industrious living that had for so long been denied them. And to prove to His Lordship, to whom the letter was addressed, that they were not the veriest beggars in the world, Secretary Pory wrote that even the cowkeeper of Jamestown came rustling to church on Sundays in flaming silk. And the wife of a man who in England had been a humble coal miner walked proudly into church as the lady of quality she had become in her rough beaver hat and a silken suit. Yes, prosperity, too, had come at last. And the settlements and plantations, large and small, were spreading over the island and beyond. There were now many private wharves up and down the James to which the big sailing vessels came regularly from England to unload supplies for the plantations and to take on the great shipments of tobacco.

Then suddenly disaster struck with the deadly swiftness of a hawk swooping down on its prey. On March 22nd of the year 1628 the colony suffered the worst Indian massacre in its history. Old Powhatan was dead and his brother Opechancanough had taken over the leadership of his tribes. Hatred for the white man had been smouldering in Opechancanough's heart for a long time and it flamed up on that morning in the brutal slaying of three hundred and forty-seven men, women and children.

The colonists had enjoyed peace for so long during Powhatan's last years that they had come to treat their Indian neighbors as friends who were often entertained in their homes with no thought of danger. So it happened that many entire families were wiped out by the Indians who had sat down to breakfast with them on the morning of that fatal day. Having been instructed by Opechancanough, they suddenly seized the colonists' own weapons and savagely murdered every member of the households in which they were staying as guests. The citizens of Jamestown escaped the massacre through the warning of a friendly Indian who had been converted to Christianity.

The settlers struck back with such fury of revenge that the savages were soon begging for peace. And for many years thereafter there was no serious trouble with the natives.

The planters turned again to peaceful pursuits and the expansion of the colony continued. When the old planters were given their dividends of land they chose acreages in various parts of the island. They were no longer confined to the cramped quarters of the old palisaded Fort which was soon to be abandoned entirely. In 1623 a surveyor laid out a new town site west of the Fort, or Old Town, and here in what was called New Town lived the governor, the officials of the colony, innkeepers, merchants and citizens. Most of the residences were of brick and most of them had gardens enclosed by palings within which vegetables, fruit and grapevines flourished. Here, too, in time the Brick Church, of which only the foundations and tower remain today, was built. The exact date of its erection is not known, but the records seem to indicate that it was planned in 1639 and was erected sometime after 1647.

In 1624 the Virginia Company of London was disbanded and Virginia became a royal colony directly under the Crown. Jamestown remained the capital and for years the little city, which was never more than a tide-washed village, struggled to become a real metropolis. Not only did it fail in this, but the town itself was doomed. The pulsing life of the colony came to be centered more and more in the ever-growing tobacco plantations along the James and the other tidewater rivers.

The last act, the last dramatic event, in the life of Jamestown was Bacon's Rebellion. In 1676 the Royal Governor, Sir William Berkeley, occupied the executive mansion in the town. And under his autocratic rule the House of Burgesses practically ceased to function. More, the Indians were on a rampage again and Governor Berkeley was taking no effective action to quell them. But love of freedom and a deep-rooted belief in the rights of the people were not dead in the colony where popular government had begun.

Rebellion against the Governor's high-handed procedures broke out and under the leadership of young Nathaniel Bacon, Jr., the people demanded redress of their wrongs and grievances. Bacon summed up their case against Governor Berkeley in a statement called "The Declaration of the People." When peaceful measures failed to bring relief from tyranny several hundred of the oppressed colonists banded together and, led by the young patriot, finally besieged Jamestown. Bacon's well-trained army was victorious and Jamestown as a stronghold of oppression was burned to the ground so that it might no longer "harbor the rogues." The Virginia colonists had learned not only to take a hand in their own government but had demonstrated both the spirit and the ability to overthrow it when it became tyrannical and opposed to the will of the people. Jamestown never recovered from this disaster and after the Statehouse burned again in 1698 the capital was moved six miles inland to Middle Plantation, a town that had developed from a private plantation and which soon afterwards changed its name to Williamsburg.

Bacon's Rebellion was a kind of dress rehearsal for the Revolution that came one hundred years later. And Bacon himself was the spiritual predecessor of that great Virginia patriot, Patrick Henry, who, one hundred years later, in the second revolutionary convention in Richmond, Virginia, shouted the immortal words: "I know not what course others may take, but as for me, give me liberty or give me death."

For a long time Americans forgot that Jamestown was the birthplace of their nation and of the liberty that its freedom-loving people have fought and died for on many battlefields. For a long time they were so busy building their great country and extending its boundaries from sea to sea that the very location of this revered spot was forgotten. But Jamestown has at last become an immortal shrine where its great and long-dead past lives again in the imagination of those who walk in reverent spirit along its haunted river bank to reconstruct the scenes that were enacted there more than three centuries ago. They hear, as did those brave settlers of so long ago, the lapping of the waters of the James, the rustling of the leaves of the cypress and the elm and the oak, the flute-like notes of birds and the winds, ancient as time, blowing through the wild woodland and over the dank swampland that was Jamestown then as it is Jamestown now.

And there is the low, but audible, whisper of ghosts for those who can hear. For those who know the history of this little island. For those who linger in the old church-yard and see something more than the empty shell of a church and the gravestones irreverently tilted by time and age. For those who in spirit can share the brave endeavor and venture of a people who came from far-distant shores across a wide, perilous ocean to found homes in a land that was savage and wild. To found first, in a little huddle of palisaded buildings, the out-post of a great empire, and then, with defiant courage, their own great nation.

That visitor to Jamestown today pays scant attention to the soaring, sky-pointed obelisk of a modern monument to the past. He hardly sees the cars parked row-on-row in a graveled parkway and the uniformed attendants who are everywhere present to tell him where to go. What he really sees, first of all, are three little ships, as bewildered as three little old ladies in a big city, looking for a safe anchorage in big Chesapeake Bay. And then he sees them bravely plowing up the broad James to the little island that was finally singled out for settlement.

And he follows them—those brave first settlers who stepped ashore off the *Discovery*, the *Sarah Constant* and the *Goodspeed*—from that first prayer beneath the blue sky of Virginia and that first night of rest on land in little tents and under bent, leafy boughs to the day when a deep-rooted colony in the New World was transplanted from its original place of settlement to a more healthful and a safer site farther inland from the James—to Williamsburg.

And having seen, so vividly in imagination, this

drama of the birth of his own great nation acted out on the hallowed ground of Jamestown Island, the visitor pauses to look thoughtfully at the statue of Captain John Smith, facing eastward down the James. How right that he should stand there, almost as though it were the Captain himself come back to the island to stay. How right that the statue of the little Indian maiden, Pocahontas, should stand near-by. Pocahontas gazing down the tree-shaded vistas up which she had so often come to Jamestown from the forest-habitation of her father, the great Powhatan. She, too, belongs to the island and seems to have come back to stay.

God rest your brave and dauntless spirits—Pocahontas and Captain John Smith.

Bibliography

Captain John Smith, Vols. I and II. Edited by EDWARD ARBER....Published by Editor, Westminster, 1884

First Republic in America, ALEXANDER BROWN.... Houghton, Mifflin Company, 1898

Historie of Travaile into Virginia Britannia, WILLIAM STRACHEY....Hakluyt Society, London, 1849

Jamestown and St. Mary's, Buried Cities of Romance, HENRY CHANDLEE FORMAN....The Johns Hopkins Press, 1938

Narratives of Early Virginia, 1606–1625. Edited by LYON GARDINER TYLER....Charles Scribner's Sons, 1907

Purchas His Pilgrimage, SAMUEL PURCHAS .... H. Fetherstone, London, 1613

Tidewater Virginia, PAUL WILSTACH....The Bobbs-Merrill Company, 1929

Travels and Works of Captain John Smith, Vols. I and II. Edited by EDWARD ARBER....J. Grant, Edinburgh, 1910

The Colonial Period of American History, Vol. I, CHARLES M. ANDREWS....Yale University Press, 1934

The First Americans, 1607–1690, THOMAS JEFFERSON WERTENBAKER....The Macmillan Company, 1927

The First Frontier, R. V. COLEMAN....Charles Scribner's Sons, 1948

The Genesis of the United States, Vols. I and II. Edited by ALEXANDER BROWN....Houghton, Mifflin Company, 1890

Bibliography

The James: From Iron Gate to the Sea, BLAIR NILES
....Rinehart and Company, 1945

The Site of Old "James Towne," 1607–1698, SAMUEL
H. YONGE....L. H. Jenkins, Inc., Richmond, 1936

The Soul of a Nation, MATTHEW PAGE ANDREWS....
Charles Scribner's Sons, 1943

*The Southern Colonies in the Seventeenth Century,
1607–1689*, WESLEY FRANK CRAVEN....Louisiana
State University Press, 1949